CLASSIC RED RATTLE

TELEGRAPH
FOR GARLIC

Samia Ounoughi is an Associate Professor at the Université
Pierre Mendés France Grenoble 2. She specializes in
character shaping/narrative structure relationships in British
nineteenth century novels and short stories, especially those
by Wilkie Collins, Mary Shelley, Robert Louis Stevenson
and Oscar Wilde. In her latest articles, she examines
solicitors and the implication of text/money circulation.

TELEGRAPH FOR GARLIC

INCLUDES
- NOTE FROM JONATHAN HARKER
- DRACULA AND THE ACADEMICS
- EXTRACTS FROM 'DRACULA'
  BY BRAM STOKER
- VAMPIRES AND AMERICAN ENTHUSIASTS
- DRACULA'S GHOST

EDITOR
SAMIA OUNOUGHI

red rattle
BOOKS

Telegraph For Garlic

2013

All published by Red Rattle Books
with the permission of the authors

Front and back cover and
artwork by Robin Castle

A CIP catalogue record for this book is
available from the British Library

ISBN 978-1-909086-08-1

Printed by Anchor Print

www.redrattlebooks.co.uk

LIST OF
CONTENTS

INTRODUCTION

'Telegraph For Garlic' is the successor to the earlier Red Rattle Books publication, 'Frankenstein Galvanized'. The two novels that have inspired this mini-series are 'Dracula' by Bram Stoker and 'Frankenstein' by Mary Shelley. Opinion is divided about the respective merit of the two books but the novels now have classic status and are culturally important because of their far-reaching influence. I hope that students, academics and the merely curious will read both 'Telegraph For Garlic' and 'Frankenstein Galvanized' and that these Red Rattle editions will not only remind them how the two novels differ from each other but perhaps explain how they provoke continued interest, new interpretations and ideas.

Mary Shelley was a radical throughout her life. When young she wandered Europe with her husband but, after Percy Shelley died, Mary settled to a self-sufficient existence with her son. This should not be a surprise. Both options offered her a form of retreat. Bram Stoker was conservative, loyal and diligent. He was gregarious and worked hard as the theatre manager of the Lyceum. He was also prepared to sacrifice some of his own ambition to support the career of his demanding boss, the actor, Sir Henry Irving. Despite the different natures of Shelley and Stoker, both writers were obliged to nurture, and probably indulge, a narcissistic male. They also created the two novels that dominate English Gothic Horror. 'Frankenstein' and 'Dracula' may be connected in the public imagination but they are separated by a good portion of a century. The first edition of 'Frankenstein' was published in 1818 and 'Dracula' appeared in 1897. Stoker is far less fearful of the modern world than Shelley but the endings of their books, the final pages, also reveal the different personalities of the two novelists. Shelley imagines the future and a family wrecked by excessive male ambition and absent female nurture. The creature is a damaged child who has never known a mother and has been rejected by the father he wanted to love. He survives the neglectful father and the past but only to wander towards an icy North Pole where he will build his funeral pyre. The warning from Shelley is clear, men and their ambition will change the world but the consequences for women and families will be horrific. Shelley has been claimed as an early feminist writer and she is because she insists upon equality and opportunity for women. But her vision of the future is not redeemed by feminism. Male scientific ambition will create wreckage because men will indulge their egos and because men without women are inadequate and destructive. Instead, the ending of 'Dracula' contained in the note by Jonathan Harker presents a happy family. Mina has helped the male warriors defeat the vampire. Her contribution is recognised by Stoker as important and she is praised in the book by all the men including Professor Van Helsing, the vampire and 'old world' expert recruited from Holland. Some critics have described Mina as the 'new woman'. But, despite her adventure, her victory has only enabled for Mina a Victorian destiny. She appears at the end of 'Dracula' as the mother to the children of Jonathan Harker. She has a family and is content. In 'Frankenstein', Mary Shelley imagines an alternative future with more secrets to be discovered and yielded but she understands that those secrets will taunt discontented and irresponsible men like Robert Walton. She is pessimistic. Stoker is different. He is the big hearted optimist who believes that providing we find men with spirit and good women to support them the present can always continue. Defeat the vampire and change can be avoided. For all its modernity and up to date technology, Stoker is unable to imagine a different future.

Both novels relish horror and they require a threat to inspire anxiety and create unease. The threat in 'Dracula' emerges from the past, the medieval world prior to the nineteenth century. Stoker only really imagines the immediate past or the present being unchanged. For him, the benefits of enlightenment need to be protected. Shelley is more imaginative and she may even be divided. She is a free spirit that values domesticity. The future, which she is obliged to welcome as a rational radical, worries her. Men are the people who have denied women opportunities. They are not the flawless noble warriors that Stoker describes. She does not want to trust them with the future, which is why she found it feasible to write the apocalyptic novel, '*The Last Man*'.

Clearly, the cinema has obscured the differences between the books. Although the novels provided memorable images for readers the cinema reproductions of the vampire and the creature have been easily transferred to bedroom walls and t-shirts. Analysts are prone to argue that '*Dracula*' is a folk tale that addresses deep fears about sex and identity and this is why it continues to be successful. The inevitability of success, though, can be overestimated. Not that long ago people were saying something similar about male identity and Westerns and then suddenly cinemagoers lost interest in cowboys and gunslingers. Without warning, primal ambitions and fears no longer guaranteed a paying audience. '*Buffy The Vampire Slayer*' has led to other vampire spin offs but it was not a success as a film and most studios were not interested in the TV series. Events and creators play a part. Without them, '*Dracula*' could have easily become a forgotten novel, and the vampire could have been a distant icon. Indeed, prior to the Hammer horror movies of the 1960s, the vampire had become a figure of fun in American cinema. At the time of their release, few fans of the Hammer films admitted to finding them chilling. Now, Hammer releases its '*Dracula*' movies on Blu-ray multiple DVD sets, and critics interpret them as essays about marriage, responsibility and fidelity. The book benefits but there are so many vampires on TV one fears that the original Dracula might be forgotten or at least not given the attention he deserves. If critics rarely claim the novel, '*Dracula*', is a masterpiece, many feel an obligation to read the book and are usually pleased that they did. Somehow, the book is essential. It belongs in the collection of serious readers.

Timing is important. The book allowed the Victorians to read about sex and persuaded them that they now lived in the modern age and in a country that was advanced and eminent in the world. This notion of Britain leading others was not new for the British but readers enjoyed it being repeated and endorsed. Van Helsing is important not because he is an expert who will predict the future. Stoker assumes that will belong to the British. The superior understanding of Professor Van Helsing relates to the past, the magic and mystery that rationalism needs to deny. This is why psychiatry has to be explained to Van Helsing by Dr Seward. For some readers today, the book may ramble, or drag in to the basic plot too many scenes from around Britain and Europe. If 'Frankenstein' feels overly thematic, we have a sense of a superior intellect being led by an imagination, a train inside the head of Mary Shelley that she is obliged to ride. Stoker is not the intellectual equal of Shelley. He is not riding a cerebral train. He is the enthusiastic boy constructing a railway set in his bedroom and, carried away by energy and zeal, he forgets to make sure that all the railway carriages match or are even needed. But whether the action takes place in Whitby Harbour, Clapham Common, London Zoo, Dr Seward's asylum or Transylvania, all the locations assure readers that Britain exists as a modern monument, especially as the tale is told by so many dedicated professionals—solicitors, doctors, scientists, zoo keepers, newspaper men and, last but not least, Mina, the 'new woman'.

So the book is different from the legends or myths that now inspire and worry people today. Stoker was willing to include anything that appealed and because of his ambition it is flawed but it does exceed most of its offspring. Of course, the vampires have changed. Unlike Stoker, modern filmmakers appear willing to embrace the future. Now, the vampire does not need to be defeated because there is no need to preserve the past. Indeed, half the fun of watching 'Buffy The Vampire Slayer' is discovering what the modern vampire thinks of the world today. What will be the surprising comment that the vampires make about TV, the teenage hangout and the latest smart phone? But, if the world and vampires have changed, some things remain constant. Our heroes may not need Christian faith anymore but they still need self-belief. Will and purpose remain important, and the heroes usually need a friend who is a constant ally. Neither have the anxieties disappeared. If anything, the modern world has made them more intense. Sexual abandonment may not be feared in quite the same way but paranoia about identity and authenticity has increased. The power of the vampire to change its form is a warning to us about our modern world. His capacity for deceit is a reminder that ambition and the need for status will conceal the motives and true thoughts of those we are obliged to trust. We should not believe what we think we see in others, indeed we cannot. All are in disguise and everyone tells lies. Today, Dracula rarely seduces virgins and despoils the Madonna needed for the Victorian home. In some instances, the women have seduced the vampire and in others they surrender willingly. They, the bad girls that parents worry about, are attracted by the prospect of superior sex and immortality. Some think they can share his power. But, apart from in the most cynical horror movies, the seduction by Dracula and any other vampire always carries a price. Not only will they have to endure relentless hunger, those he seduces will have aspects of themselves revealed that they would rather not see. The monster inside them will emerge. So, the paranoia in the vampire myth and book is powerful and relevant. It tells us that we neither recognize others nor ourselves. While these fears should keep us all awake at night their existence is no guarantee that the vampire phenomenon has to continue for as long as we create fiction. For the moment, though, most of us including film producers and publishers are hedging our bets. The vampire is behaving as if he expects to have the future predicted by his legend.

The title of this book, *'Telegraph For Garlic'*, is intended to be a tribute to the determination, foresight and fortitude of Professor Van Helsing. He admonishes Lucy for thinking that he is playing a trick on her by putting garlic in her room. The Professor explains to Lucy, *'I had to telegraph yesterday, or they would not have been here.'*[1] Unfortunately, the prompt arrival of the garlic was not enough to save poor Lucy.

This book complements the Red Rattle edition of *'Frankenstein Galvanized'*. As with the previous book we have mixed the analysis

---

1   Stoker, Bram, *'Dracula'*, Oxford University Press, Edition 2011, page 123.

by the academics with comment from an enthusiast. The academics are based in England and France and their analysis is restricted to the novel by Stoker. Their interests include the philosophical and social – madness, religion, superstition and politics - , the personal – the misunderstood nature of Lucy Westenra - and the specific and technical – text and blood as a metaphor and the relationship of technology to supernatural identity. Howard Jackson is currently preparing an anthology of his own horror stories, which will be published by Red Rattle in 2014. He examines a book and a film that feature vampires other than Dracula.

The essays by the academics are intended for students and general readers although some readers will find some of the essays more accessible than others. As we stated in *'Frankenstein Galvanized'*, the more difficult can be understood if they are read twice or carefully. The analysis by Howard Jackson does not require academic expertise and can serve as a way of relaxing after the more demanding analysis that exists in other parts of the book. Also included in the book are extracts from the original novel by Bram Stoker, and his short story, *'Dracula's Guest'*. The extracts are intended to emphasise some of the points made in the essays in *'Dracula And The Academics'*. They also highlight what are effective and interesting elements within the book by Stoker and provide some idea of the various voices that Stoker used to draft his novel. Some of the extracts selected do not begin with dates in the novel. Dates have been added and are in the brackets above the extract. This should make the chronology clear. Florence Stoker, the mother of Bram Stoker, claimed that *'Dracula's Guest'* was an unpublished episode from *'Dracula'*. Bram Stoker removed it because of the length of the book.

We had intended to include the complete novel by Stoker as happened with the Red Rattle book, *'Frankenstein Galvanized'*, but on that occasion it was felt that a different print layout would add to the experience of reading the novel by Shelley. *'Dracula'* is already available in an excellent edition by Oxford University Press. The approach taken with *'Telegraph For Garlic'* means that we can make the academic comment and analysis available at an economic price and not only give some idea of the novel but perhaps help readers think differently about the achievement of Stoker.

Anyone who has any queries about *'Telegraph For Garlic'* or would like to make suggestions for future editions can contact the Red Rattle Books website www.redrattlebooks.co.uk. Comments are also welcome.

NOTES ON
CONTRIBUTORS

Marion Sones-Marceau is a senior lecturer at Paris Dauphine. She has written about the link between literature and society, involving the development of the book market, writers responsibilities and the effects of social crisis. She has had works published by the Presses de l'Université de Paris Sorbonne, Les Chaiers du CICLaS and Ashgate Publishing.

Helena Ifill teaches English Literature at the University of Sheffield. Her research concerns the intersections between Victorian literature and science writing, particularly focusing on depictions of insanity, heredity, degeneracy and pseudo-sciences such as mesmerism in sensation fiction of the 1860s and the urban Gothic. She has also written about the ways in which medical writing engaged with Victorian gender debates.

Claire Bazin is Professor of nineteenth century and Commonwealth Literature at Paris Ouest Nanterre la Défense. She has published 2 books on Charlotte Brontë's *'Jane Eyre'* and 2 on New Zealand writer Janet Frame as well as a number of articles on Mary Shelley's *'Frankenstein'* and Bram Stoker's *'Dracula'*.

Jean-Jacques Lecercle is Emeritus Professor of English at the Université de Paris in Nanterre. A specialist of Victorian literature and the philosophy of language, he has published, among others, *'Philosophy of Nonsense', 'Interpretation As Pragmatics', 'A Marxist Philosophy of Language'* and *'Badiou and Deleuze Read Literature'*.

Samia Ounoughi is an Associate Professor at the Université Pierre Mendés France Grenoble 2. She specializes in character shaping/narrative structure relationships in British nineteenth century novels and short stories, especially those by Wilkie

Collins, Mary Shelley, Robert Louis Stevenson and Oscar Wilde. In her latest articles, she examines solicitors and the implication of text/money circulation.

R J E Riley is a Lecturer in English (post-1900) at the University of Cambridge. He has recently edited two collections linked to the archives of novelist and filmmaker, Peter Whitehead, and has written on terrorism, cult film and conspiracy for Vertigo, *'One+One'* and *'Transgressive Culture'*. He maintains a blog at http://residual-noise.blogspot.co.uk/

Howard Jackson has written *'Treat Me Nice'*, *'Innocent Mosquitoes'* and *'No Money Honey'*. His blog *'Stagecoach To Somewhere'* contains horror fiction, news from Brazil and music and film reviews. He reviews crime fiction for 'Crime Chronicles'. *'Treat Me Nice'* compares the life of Elvis Presley to that of the Frankenstein creature. *'Innocent Mosquitoes'* describes an 11,000 mile journey around Brazil.

NOTE FROM
JONATHAN HARKER

NOTE

Seven years ago we all went through the flames; and the happiness of some of us since then is, we think, well worth the pain we endured. It is an added joy to Mina and to me that our boy's birthday is the same day as that on which Quincey Morris died. His mother holds, I know, the secret belief that some of our brave friend's spirit has passed into him. His bundle of names links all our little band of men together; but we call him Quincey.

In the summer of this year we made a journey to Transylvania, and went over the old ground which was, and is, to us so full of vivid and terrible memories. It was almost impossible to believe that the things which we had seen with our own eyes and heard with our own ears were living truths. Every trace of all that had been was blotted out. The castle stood as before, reared high above a waste of desolation.

When we got home we got to talking of the old time—which we could all look back on without despair, for Godalming and Seward are both happily married. I took the papers from the safe where they have been ever since our return so long ago. We were struck with the fact that, in all the mass of material of which the record is composed, there is hardly one authentic document! nothing but a mass of type-writing, except the later note-books of Mina and Seward and myself, and Van Helsing's memorandum. We could hardly ask anyone, even did we wish to, to accept these as proofs of so wild a story. Van Helsing summed it all up as he said, with our boy on his knee:—

'We want no proofs; we ask none to believe us! This boy will some day know what a brave and gallant woman his mother is. Already he knows her sweetness and loving care; later on he will understand how some men so loved her, that they did dare much for her sake.'

JONATHAN HARKER

DRACULA AND
THE ACADEMICS

DRACULA: THE GOTHIC RESURRECTED

MARION SONES-MARCEAU

DRACULA:
THE GOTHIC RESURRECTED

The literary genre of Gothic was born in 1764 with Horace Walpole's *'The Castle of Otranto'*. Its initial evolution lasted little more than fifty years, culminating in the creation of Mary Shelley's iconic *'Frankenstein'* in 1818. Whilst that milestone had seemed likely to give rise to immediate further expansion of the genre, in fact it was to take nearly another eighty years for the Gothic to once again find prominence. It was in 1897 that Bram Stoker sprung *'Dracula'* into life. In truth, the Gothic had hardly survived the intervening period between what are now considered its two primary icons. How did such a spectacular revival come about? For, indeed, it was something that propelled the genre to the heights of a permanent literary fixture.

The origins of the Gothic novel are bound closely to the origins of the English novel itself. The birth of the novel in England can be traced back to the beginning of the 18th century. The elitism of literature was being challenged by the emergence of a new and literate middle class. As the century continued and the Industrial Revolution delivered its benefits this new readership grew in size. The middle class wanted literature that reflected its own values and was prepared to pay for it as soon as it became available. A market for books was being born and the first commercial publishers were those shrewd enough to see the business potential. By 1750, two genres led the charge towards this expanded market. They were the sentimental, which was dominated by Samuel Richardson, and the picaresque, the most famous example being *'Tom Jones'* by Henry Fielding. The sentimental concentrated on the expression of deep feelings and emotions whilst the picaresque touched upon the lighter side of life through the wanderings of a central character. Both genres tapped into prevailing moods of the day. When, therefore, these changed, becoming heavier and regressive in the later part of the century, literature was forced to reflect this shift. Gothic filled that need. It explored the darker side of the soul; three levels of intensity evolved, fear, terror and horror. Fear and terror novels started the trend, horror followed. The latter, the most intense, did not appear until after the relative decline of the former two. Sophia Lee's *'The Recess'* (1783-85) epitomized the Gothic in its milder form of fear, its presence being diluted by that of an emotional softness. With authors such as Horace Walpole, Clara Reeve and Ann Radcliffe, the fear factor was intensified to become one of terror. By the time Shelley produced *'Frankenstein'*, the Gothic had become full-blooded horror as in M. G. Lewis's *'The Monk'* (1796). But this was where the genre, particularly in that last dramatic form, was about to fade in popularity. The mood of the country was changing yet again. As a consequence, after 1818, *'Melmoth the Wanderer'* (1820) might be the only major work able to justify a label of authentic Gothic.

For the next fifty years, the Gothic was to be buried under the avalanche of the Victorian novel although critics have sought to mention certain Gothic elements within the writings of Dickens and the Brontë sisters amongst others. A new Queen had come to the throne in 1837 and this had both helped define a new age and herald the progress that was being made. The move to a modern urban economy based on manufacturing and trade to replace one of land ownership brought about wealth and success. The Industrial Revolution in full swing was producing advancements like steam power, the telegraph, photography and many other useful inventions. Free trade broadened consumer choice. The stunning Crystal Palace exhibition in 1851 displayed British greatness. Money and power meant education for everybody. Even political freedom was advanced, with the First Reform Bill (1832) giving voting rights to the middle classes, and the Second Reform Bill (1867) extending these rights to the working classes. The Empire was at its height with Britain controlling no less than a quarter of the world.

In literature, there was a recognition that a new readership, which included all categories of the population, was looking for guidance and edification from the works of their authors, rather than exploration into the dark fears of past centuries typified by the Gothic. From each decade emerged one or more celebrated novelist. The 30's produced the earliest Dickens works, the 40's those of the Brontë sisters. The 50's saw William M. Thackaray ('*Vanity Fair*') challenging Dickens whilst the 60's were marked by the prominence of Anthony Trollope ('*Barchester Towers*'). In the 70's, George Eliot added her name to the illustrious list. Her novels included her masterpiece, '*Middlemarch*'. Successful authors of this period were examining contemporary England and its society. Generally, they stayed close to the realism of the day, and usually the writing had a puritanical edge. Whilst the subject of money was often at the forefront, it was put forward in the context of social responsibility.

The remnants of the Gothic in England were almost confined to unsophisticated publications such as penny dreadfuls. These cheap magazines (the forerunners of the modern day weekly comics) serialized certain Gothic horror tales alongside stories about crime and criminals. They were aimed at the working class. The most successful of these is considered to be '*The Mysteries of London*' (1844) by George W. M. Reynolds.

But beyond 1870, the geopolitical map was beginning to change once again. Britain, the dominant force and influence in the world, started to sense threats. Strength was building in the USA but it was the powers much closer to home that were giving greatest causes for concern. The rise of the Austro-Hungarian Empire (created in 1867) and of the formalization of Germany into a unified nation state in 1871 dampened the free spirit of the British. They started to turn inwards upon themselves as they had done at the end of the previous century. Although exciting and positive adventure stories such as H. Rider Haggard's '*King Solomon's Mines*' (1885) were still popular, the marketplace was starting to see a rise in literary works, which explored a more sinister side of life. Books such as '*Dr Jekyll and Mr Hyde*' (1886) by Robert Louis Stevenson or '*The Picture of Dorian Gray*' (1890) by Oscar Wilde examined evil as a concept. Whilst these were important, a new genre was gaining ground with British readers. It was the genre of the 'invasion'. Interest in the genre was substantial and 400 books were produced in a short time, starting with G. T. Chesney's *'Battle of Dorking'* (1871), a story of Germanic invasion of England. The fear of invasion reflected perfectly the British concerns that prevailed in this period. It was different from the fear of the *'Frankenstein'* era, which was one of evil from within. Invasion was a fear of evil from without, since it included the threat from immigration, which, led by ever-increasing numbers from Ireland and Eastern Europe, was starting to be felt by the population. In its finest form, it produced H.G. Wells' classic, *'War of the Worlds'*, in 1898.

The vampire concept allied itself beautifully to that of invasion, since it vividly represented a terrible invasion of the body. The vampire character was created by William Polidori at the same time and place as Mary Shelley's *'Frankenstein'*. Its next significant appearance was with J. M. Rymer's *'Varney the Vampire'* (1845-47) but this happened initially only in the 'dreadful' magazines. The mood of fear in England opened the way for the vampire's return yet again, this time in female form with J. S. Le Fanu's *'Carmilla'* in 1872. But it was Stoker, some fifteen years later, who found the grand key to maximizing its effect. He used the Gothic element of historical backdrop (Dracula's Transylvanian castle) to set the tone and then brought the story into the contemporary era by having the vampire operating in modern-day England. This transposition of Gothic horror was stunningly relevant, dramatic and terrifying. The book was immediately successful.

Dracula's elevation to iconic status, however, didn't really happen until after Stoker's death. It was Dracula's suitability to the newly created cinema industry in the early 20th century that both immortalized the character and simultaneously resurrected the whole Gothic genre that is still happening today.

Bibliography

Carré, Jacques.' *La Grande-Bretagne au XIXe siècle'*, Hachette Supérieur, Paris (1997)

Johnson, Allan. *'Modernity and Anxiety in Bram Stoker's Dracula'* in Critical Insights: *'Dracula'* by Bram Stoker, Salem Press, Pasadena (2010): 72-84

Keech, James R. *'The Survival of the Gothic Response'* Studies in the Novel 6 (1974): 130-144.

Mayo Robert D. *'How Long was Gothic Fiction in Vogue?'* Modern Language Notes 48 (1943): 58-64.

Varma, Devendra P. *'The Gothic Flame'*, Russell & Russell, New York (1957)

'SWEETER AND LOVELIER THAN EVER'
RE-READING LUCY

HELENA IFILL

'SWEETER AND
LOVELIER THAN EVER'
RE-READING LUCY

'Why can't they let a girl marry three men, or as many as want her, and save all this trouble? But this is heresy, and I must not say it'. (Lucy Westenra)[1]

This comment by Lucy Westenra to her correspondent and confidante, Mina Murray, from *'Dracula'* by Bram Stoker has been frequently discussed by critics but the range of opinion expressed has been disappointingly narrow. The recurring interpretation of Lucy's words is that her apparent flippancy masks a desire (more or less subconscious) not only to marry but to sexually possess *'three men, or as many as want her'*(59). Subsequently, her later transformation into a 'voluptuous' vampire is somehow punishment for, or an ironic playing out of, this desire.[2] This reading can be found in a range of critical works from the last few decades. Geoffrey Wall (1984) refers to Lucy's *'heretically polygamous wish'*[3]; Kathleen L. Spencer (1992) has asserted that *'we sense that she means what she says; she really would like to marry all of them'*[4]; Andrew Smith (2004) has argued that Lucy's words suggest a *'latent desire for promiscuity'.*[5] Most recently (2012), Tanya Pikula has used Lucy's words as evidence for identifying the character *'with forms of unrestrained consumption'* and sees her as *'craving far more men than the traditional, heterosexual marriage can decently*

1   Bram Stoker, *'Dracula'* (Oxford: Oxford University Press, 1998), 59. All further references are to this edition and in the main body of the essay.

2   Stoker, *'Dracula'*, 214. The word is used repeatedly in connection to both Lucy and the female vampires in Dracula's castle.

3   Geoffrey Wall, *'Different from Writing': Dracula in 1897'* In *'Bloom's Modern Critical Interpretations: Bram Stoker's Dracula'*, edited by Harold Bloom (Philadelphia: Chelsea House, 2003), 27-38 (34).

4   Kathleen L. Spencer *'Purity and Danger: Dracula, the Urban Gothic, and the Late Victorian Degeneracy Crisis.'* ELH 59, no. 1 (Spring 1992): 197-225 (210).

5   Andrew Smith, *'Victorian Demons: Medicine, Masculinity and the Gothic at the Fin-de-Siècle'* (Manchester: Manchester University Press, 2004), 145. Also from the 2000s we have Ken Gelder (2001) explaining that *'Lucy reveals through her letters to Mina that she already has a sexual 'appetite'—as if her transformation into a vampire later on simply makes manifest what was privately admitted between friends'*. Ken Gelder, *'Reading the Vampire'* (London: Routledge, 2001), 77.

accommodate'.[6] Such readings of Lucy reach their culmination in Francis Ford Coppola's *'Bram Stoker's Dracula'* in which Lucy is shown to be a consummate flirt and whose transformation into a vampire is depicted in hypersexual scenes; in fact *'former porn queen Traci Lords was mentioned as a contender for the role'.*[7] The message is made clear that Lucy is a highly sexed young woman and that Dracula merely encourages these tendencies.

These readings of Lucy, which conflate sex and marriage, often contribute to the body of *'Dracula'* criticism which connects it with perverse, aggressive, transgressive and excessive sexuality, reading into the novel acts of *'rape (including gang rape), aggressive female sexuality, fellatio, homoeroticism, incest, bestiality, necrophilia, paedophilia, and sexually transmitted disease..'*[8] By returning to the text and looking at what Lucy actually says, and the context in which she says it, alternative interpretations may emerge. Lucy's words do not need to be seen as an acknowledgement (unconscious or otherwise) of promiscuous desire. They reveal a young Victorian woman's ignorance of what the state of marriage entails. Alongside other letters between Lucy and Mina, it becomes clear that, rather than secretly craving many men, Lucy is shown to be anxious about how to manage one man, let alone three. This novel has usually, and for some perfectly good reasons, been read as *'by a man, about men and for men'*[9] but Lucy's experience in the novel, particularly after she has become a vampire, can in fact be read as a nightmare literalization of women's fears that they may not prove adequate as wives and mothers.[10] This in turn is attached to nineteenth century anxieties about the security and sanctity of the household and the vulnerability of the wife—the person who (according to standard

6   Tanya Pikula, 'Bram Stoker's Dracula and Late-Victorian Advertising Tactics: Earnest Men, Virtuous Ladies, and Porn,' ELT 55:3 (2012): 289. Other readings include Andrew Smith. These readings have influenced adaptations such as Francis Ford Coppola's film.

7   David K. Skal, 'Hollywood Gothic: The Tangled Web of 'Dracula' From Novel to Stage to Screen', revised (New York: Faber and Faber, 2004), 281.

8   Elizabeth Miller, 'Coitus Interruptus: Sex, Bram Stoker, and Dracula', Romanticism on the Net 44 (November, 2006).

9   Fred Botting, 'Dracula, Romance and Radcliffean Gothic', Women's Writing 1:2 (1994): 181-201 (181).

10 For discussion of earlier Gothic works as literalizations of women's condition see Ruth Bienstock Anolik, 'The Missing Mother: The Meanings of Maternal Absence in the Gothic Mode', Modern Language Studies 33:1/2 (Spring-Autumn 2003):26.

Victorian ideals) should act as the moral heart of the family. Perverse sexuality is not the trigger for terror here—the prospect of a traditional marriage is the real cause for Lucy's concern.

Let us turn to Lucy's (supposedly) ill-fated words and look at the context in which she utters them. When Lucy asks '*why can't they let a girl marry three men, or as many as want her, and save all this trouble*' this is actually a defensively flippant response to an upsetting event (59). Lucy has just rejected her second suitor of the day (Quincey Morris) but also accepted the man she loves, Arthur Holmwood. We already know that, despite her admiration of her first two suitors, Lucy only has eyes for Arthur. When first mentioning John Seward in a letter Lucy claims that he would '*just do for*' Mina (54). When describing Quincey's proposal she begins to admit that she is impressed by his stories of his adventures and admits '*I know now what I would do if I were a man and wanted to make a girl love me*' but she then checks herself: '*No, I don't, for there was Mr Morris telling us his stories, and Arthur never told any, and yet—*' (57). She also rejects the other suitors before Arthur's proposal; he is her first and only choice of husband. In the opening of her letter to Mina it is clear that she is emotionally torn between being '*so happy that I don't know what to do with myself*' and feeling '*sorry, really and truly sorry, for two of the poor fellows*' (56) whom she likes and respects. She actually has to stop writing after describing her rejection of Dr Seward as she feels '*so miserable*' despite being '*so happy*' (57). Whilst she is certainly flattered by the attention and admits to '*feeling a sort of exultation that* [Quincey] *was number two in one day*', she is sincerely sorry at having caused so much pain (58).

Rather than making a ribald reference to having multiple sexual partners, Lucy actually reveals an innocent unawareness of what being married to three men would really entail.[11] This joke works differently on the homo-and the heterodiegetic levels and also (broadly) for married and unmarried Victorian readers. Lucy consciously makes what she sees as a mildly risqué quip about

---

11 Some discussion of the famous polyandrous blood transfusions and the 'gang-rape' staking of vampire Lucy is necessary here. Rather than Lucy getting what she wished for, I would read this as the men getting what they have wanted all along – Lucy.

accepting three proposals in order to cover her own discomfort at causing the men pain, readers who have knowledge or experience of married life realise the sexual implications of what she is saying and can find humour in her innocence. The joke is only effective if Lucy is unaware of what she is saying. Lucy's sudden checking of herself after she makes her comment (*'but this is heresy, and I must not say it'*(59)) also works on two levels—it is an acknowledgement that she has just said something slightly inappropriate but also a sign as to how seriously, even in jest, she is now taking her role as an affianced young lady. This combination of innocence and a desire to fulfil her role as a wife effectively becomes the signature tone in Lucy's fate, both before and after her vamping by Dracula.

The knowledge and experience of unmarried Victorian women (even within the same class) varied massively depending on personal circumstance. Certainly, many middle- and upper-class women would have had little sex education as *'respectable parents believed that ignorance of sex would keep their daughters pure'*.[12] Yet, whilst some young women may have entertained *'a hazy idea of loving and being loved, in a warm glow of cuddles and kisses'*[13] much literature was available to burst any such bubbles. The eighteenth and nineteenth centuries had seen numerous intense discussions, debates and arguments over the role of women, the responsibilities of wives and mothers and the way in which women should prepare or be prepared for marriage. Regardless of whether writings were conservative or radical, political or popular, there was a dominant message that the role of wife and mother (particularly the latter) was sacred, challenging and to be taken seriously. In 1792, Mary Wollstonecraft used the fact that *'the care of children in their infancy is one of the grand duties annexed to the female character by nature'* in order to *'afford many forcible arguments for strengthening the female understanding.'*[14] A century later, an advice manual for women insisted that *'in the*

---

12 Joan Perkin, 'Victorian Women' (London: John Murray, 1993), 52.

13 Perkin, 'Victorian Women', 52.

14 Mary Wollstonecraft, 'A Vindication of the Rights of Woman.' Bartleby.com. 1792. http://www.bartleby.com/144/10.html (accessed February 28, 2013), 5.

performance of her heaven-intrusted [sic] task she is fulfilling a mission so lofty and so sacred that none other can ever approach to it'.[15] At the same time, there was the generally expressed belief that *'female education, as conducted in the present day [...] fails to prepare the* character, *and to form the habits'* for married life.[16] For any young Victorian woman who read even a small portion of the literature available in a range of forms, there was enough to engender anxiety at the prospect of marriage and uncertainty as to her own ability to cope. Whilst Lucy is not shown to read or discuss any such literature, the pervasiveness of it in the nineteenth century zeitgeist suggests how much value and pressure was placed on the married woman. Lucy's situation reflects that of many educated young women who had been taught that marriage and motherhood was to be their greatest achievement in life but who possessed *'little to no sexual experience'* and little understanding of what embarking on married life really meant.[17]

Lucy has been read by some as an embodiment of one end of the spectrum of the New Woman—the sexually promiscuous end. She is in fact a traditional girl at heart who throws herself sincerely into becoming an *'old married wom[a]n'*, insisting to Mina that *'a woman ought to tell her husband everything—don't you think so dear?'* (56). At the same time we can see some anxiety that she may not be able to live up to the required standard: *'men like women, certainly their wives, to be quite as fair as they are; and women, I am afraid, are not always quite so fair as they should be'* (ibid). Lucy worries about her own morality based on what she thinks men expect; she does not even know enough to specify what Arthur wants, but must generalize based on her sketchy knowledge of gender stereotypes. It does not make things easier that at this period in history those stereotypes were, like many other former certainties, undergoing destabilization:

---

15 Kellogg, quoted in Mrs. John Thompson, *'Special Supplement to Vol. I Maiden, Wife, and Mother: or to The Ladies' Guide'*. London: L.N. Fowler, 1891, 48.

16 Sarah Stickney Ellis, *'The Wives of England: Their Relative Duties, Domestic Influence, and Social Obligations'*. New York: Appleton, 1843, 36.

17 Jennifer Phegley, *'Courtship and Marriage in Victorian England'* (Santa Barbara, California: Praeger, 2012), 139.

The pressures on middle-class Victorians to conform were intense [...], while the model to which they were required to conform was losing its clarity. The old consensus on the central distinctions of their society on which distinctions were indeed central, and on how those distinctions were to be defined and maintained-was breaking down.[18]

Soon after her declaration about what '*men like*', Lucy begins to think more specifically about Arthur as an individual and wonders about the extent to which she will have to modify her own behaviour once married: '*I do not know myself if I shall ever speak slang: I do not know if Arthur likes it*' (58). Considering Lucy's fascination with slang and her own tentative use of it, this shows an unquestioning willingness to conform to Arthur's desires but also some latent concern as to what that might involve.[19] Privileged, protected and frivolous (certainly compared to the dutiful and industrious Mina), Lucy nevertheless does her best to prepare herself for the solemnity of marriage.

So Lucy's happy anticipation of her marriage, masking potential anxiety about what she is letting herself in for, reflects the uncertainties of young women who were aware of the sacred state into which they were entering but had no idea what married life would really be like. Her post-vamped state depicts a nightmare scenario in which all her unformed fears come true. Although there is no actual wedding, Lucy's reference to Arthur as her husband (211) and Arthur's claim that he feels they are married after the blood transfusion (174) moves this part of the book into the '*honeymoon Gothic*' genre.[20] As with everything concerning Lucy from this point on, the marriage between Lucy and Arthur sort of happens but not in the way it should do. Critical readings such as those cited at the start of this essay have linked Lucy's

---

18 Spencer, 'Purity and Danger', 207.

19 Stoker, 'Dracula', 55, 58. The fact that Lucy's musings focus on slang, linguistically outside the norm, mildly shocking, may indeed hint at her willingness, perhaps even desire, to experiment in other areas of her life. Once again, however, I would resist jumping to the assumption that this must mean some form of hidden extreme sexual perversion – Lucy may get a thrill from declaring that '*dress is a bore*' (55) but she remains well within the bounds of socially acceptable behaviour. The reader could hardly imagine her swearing, for example!

20 Helena Michie, 'Victorian Honeymoons: Journeys to the Conjugal' (Cambridge: Camuridge University Press, 2006).

development into a 'voluptuous' vampire with a new aggressive sexuality and promiscuity on her part. However, we can see that even in her corrupted state, which clearly makes her 'unfit'[21] to perform such a role, Lucy attempts to act as a wife and mother.

Many critics have seen Lucy in her vampire state as a perversion of maternity. Phyllis Roth's early (1977) reading of Lucy represents her as a mother figure with whom the male characters' *'desire to do away'* because she is *'desirable [...] sexual [...] threatening'*.[22] More recently Smith has argued that

> *'Stoker uses Lucy Westenra's transformation as the 'bloofar [sic] lady' who preys on working-class children, in order to demonise a particular form of inverted motherhood, one in which she suckles children'.*[23]

Leslie Ann Minot, contrastingly, has read Lucy against Victorian discourses of *'child sexual victimization'*.[24] Gelder also discusses the connections between Lucy's behaviour and child molestation, casually adding that *'at least one child enjoys the experience'* but not taking this any further. Still, this is something to consider—perhaps the children enjoyed being taken by Lucy not because she is an abuser but because she treats them well. Without the narrative of Lucy, we have no proof as to what Lucy does with the children beyond biting them but the suggestion is that she does not scare them as one child wants to 'play' with her again (195).

There are several possible readings here which, whilst not denying Lucy's vampiric nature, suggest that she sees the children as more than midnight snacks. Lucy is clearly taking enough blood to survive but not draining them to any serious extent. We know from the vampire hunters' encounter with Lucy that she takes the children to her tomb (215) but afterwards she takes the

---

21 Smith, 'Victorian Demons', 145.

22 Phyllis A. Roth, 'Suddenly Sexual Women in Bram Stoker's Dracula', ed by Harold Bloom (Philadelphia: Chelsea House, 2003), 3-14 (p.9).

23 Smith, 'Victorian Demons', 145.

24 Leslie-Ann Minot, 'Vamping the Children: The 'Bloofer Lady', the 'London Minotaur' and 'Child-Victimisation in Late Nineteenth-Century England', in 'Victorian Crime, Madness and Sensation', ed by Andrew Maunder and Grace Moore (Aldershot: Ashgate, 2004):207-18 (207).

time to return them to Hampstead Heath (178) where they can be found and cared for. Another possible consideration is that Lucy is unsuccessfully attempting to 'turn' the children that she takes. As Minot observes, *'the bite of the vampire also has the quality of contagion or conversion—that is, turns the victim into a vampire'.*[25] Lucy has recently turned into a vampire, is possibly abandoned by Dracula (we know several of his boxes were taken from Carfax after his final attack on Lucy (156)), and is uncertain how the whole 'vamping' process works due to her semi-unconscious state during Dracula's attacks. Whilst Minot suggests that there is *'a threat of sexual recruitment'* in Lucy's behaviour, I would argue that she is trying to procreate as best she can. Van Helsing clearly fears this possibility as he is concerned that the child in the hospital should not be allowed to *'remain out another night'* as *'it would probably be fatal'* (196).

It was generally assumed that women would want to have children and that they would take to it naturally. As one advice book from 1891 asserted:

'The motherly instinct is the ruling passion in every true woman. In no sphere does woman shine to such advantage, or show her God-given graces of character so well, as when fulfilling her duties of nurturing and training for usefulness and goodness the plastic minds of the little ones that have been entrusted to her care'.[26]

Barrenness, contrastingly, was *'a most undesirable condition of family affairs, and one that should be avoided by all who can be parents'.*[27] This was a lot of pressure for young women to face. There is certainly a perversion of the maternal role here, as Lucy must feed from children, rather than providing nourishment for them but her behaviour actually suggests that even in her vampire state she is trying to act as a mother. Lucy is clutching the child

25   Minot, 'Vamping the Children', 211.

26   Thompson, Mrs. John,' Special Supplement to Vol. I Maiden, Wife, and Mother': or to 'The Ladies' Guide'. London: L.N. Fowler, 1891, 48.

27   Thompson, 52-3.

'*strenuously to her breast*' when the vampire hunters see her (211), a pose which could suggest breast feeding. Yet, when she sees Arthur, her fiancé whom she had hoped would provide her with legitimate children of her own, she drops the stolen child and approaches him: '*Come to me, Arthur. Leave these others and come to me. My arms are hungry for you. Come, and we can rest together. Come, my husband, come!*'[28]

Wall refers to Arthur as Lucy's '*cheated lover*' but the fact that Lucy only approaches Arthur suggests that she is not wanton or promiscuous; she is asking the man who should have been her husband to come to her.[29]

Perhaps not unreasonably, Arthur (initially revolted by the sight of a bloodstained Lucy with a stolen child) is drawn by the '*languorous, voluptuous grace*' with which Lucy approaches him: '*moving his hands from his face, he opened wide his arms*' until Van Helsing raises the crucifix before her, revealing her demonic side (211-12). Van Helsing's intervention may seem extreme as he attempts to separate husband and wife. Lucy's desire for Arthur is not clearly excessive. It is appropriate for a young bride who desires to be a mother. Lucy's flaunted sexuality may be '*too much*' by Victorian standards but it is neither promiscuous nor polygamous. Her excitement at the idea of marriage may certainly include excitement about the upcoming wedding night, or more likely (based on her eagerness to please as demonstrated previously) an anxiousness to perform as Arthur will expect and like. Lucy's new voluptuous appearance and attitude may be read as both her anticipation of the pleasures of marriage and her transformation into the kind of woman that she believes Arthur will want. In her innocent former life, she has learnt from Quincey that men desire to be kissed—a gesture which makes her blush but which she performs to make him feel better (59)—and in her new vampiric form she offers to kiss her fiancé (161). Robbed of her wedding, her wedding night and her wedded life, the vampiric Lucy

---

28 Stoker, '*Dracula*', 211. As Gelder mentions, vampire Lucy's '*behaviour is always represented to us by men*' and it is Seward who '*judges Lucy as 'cold-blooded*' in her '*treatment of the sleeping child*' (75).

29 Wall, '*Different from Writing*', 35.

still clings to the hopes and dreams of her innocent human self.

But if we continue to read this novel as a form of Honeymoon Gothic, the desire with which Arthur responds to Lucy is inappropriate when contextualized alongside contemporary advice-literature. One early twentieth century manual warned that *'marriage is by no means 'legalised licentiousness.'* [...] *'To act in the marriage bed like the beasts that perish is to rob married life of its joy and peace.'*[30] Similarly, an 1891 advice manual warned that the sole object of sexual congress is clearly generation. It has no other end or purpose. When God created man and woman with a dual sexuality his design was evidently to enable them to propagate their kind, not that they might unite for mere sexual pleasure.[31]

The author suggests sex causes the loss of 'energy' in both parties and she informs [rather than reminds] them that they cannot afford to waste *'a very vital fluid, called semen'*. She goes on to warn that *'many young people go to great excesses sexually, especially during the first months of their married life'* and describes the 'sickly' babies that are the result.[32] A man, we are told, will lose the 'desire' for *'a close and high spiritual intimacy with a woman whom he uses principally as an instrument of animal passion'*.[33] Lucy's new look (*'more radiantly beautiful than ever'* (200), yet displaying *'adamantine, heartless cruelty'* (211)) sparks a desire which is excessive in conservative Victorian eyes and which temporarily causes Arthur to disregard his moral response to her new state as a child abductor. He is, at least as Seward describes it, overtaken by lust and seems *'under a spell'* (212). One dominant image of the ideal married Victorian woman, particularly as promoted by much medical writing (most famously that of William Acton), was of an 'asexual' being who did not shock *'public feeling with a display of sexual desire'*.[34] As Smith

---

30 A. Dennison Light, 'Marriage: Before and After' (London: Health & Vim, n.d. (c.1910)), 34.

31 Thompson,' Special Supplement', 55.

32 Thompson, 'Special Supplement', 55-6. A similar warning is given in Light's 'Marriage': 'Do you ask me what is excess? I think you can guess what my answer will be. It is this, whenever you indulge in sexual connection, apart from the object of parenthood, you commit excess', A. Dennison Light, 'Marriage: Before and After' (London: Health & Vim, n.d. (c.1910)), 36.

33 Thompson, 'Man's Sexual Relations', quoted in Thompson, 'Special Supplement', 57.

34 Frank Mort, 'Dangerous Sexualities: Medico-Moral Politics in England since 1830', 2nd edn (London: Routledge, 2000), 62-3.

argues, *'what is truly horrific to the vampire hunters is the transformation not the ostensible fact that she is a vampire'.*[35] The new vampiric Lucy is too attractive, too sexual and too little like the ideal image of the suitable wife. The response she provokes in the men is one which cannot be allowed to take control.

Lucy has unknowingly been possessed symbolically by other men. Arthur, her true love, is disgusted at her attempts to please him. Later, he penetrates her violently in a manner that brings death rather than life. And Lucy is unable to nourish the children that she clutches to her breast. All this makes the vampiric afterlife of Lucy not a release of aggressive or perverse female sexuality but a Gothic playing out of a young woman's concerns about embarking on marriage. Stoker is tapping into the fears of a society which both idolized the wife and mother but also worried that she was vulnerable, corruptible and that her degeneration (physical, mental or moral) would destroy the entire family. We do not have to turn to extreme transgressive sexuality in order to discover a key horror within *'Dracula'*. Nor do we have to delve particularly deep into the unconscious. *'Dracula'* is a novel which focuses on young people about to embark on a new stage of life, one that was revered by the society in which Stoker and his readers were raised. It is a horror story for anyone who has experienced, or imagined, the excitement and trepidation of finding suitable (i.e. socially-sanctioned) love and has been faced with the risks and responsibilities it brings.

---

35   Smith,145.

RELIGION, SUPERSTITION AND MADNESS IN 'DRACULA'

CLAIRE BAZIN

RELIGION
AND SUPERSTITION

God

'Dracula' abounds in religious references and appeals to God almost ad nauseam: *'God help us all'* (153), *'God help us all'* (173), *'Please the good God'* (181), etc. It is too religiously correct. When Jonathan is travelling to Transylvania telling the people he meets about his destination they keep crossing themselves or sporting crucifixes as their weapons against Evil. Superstition and religion are closely intertwined as both resort to the same symbols or objects, such as crucifixes. The later trip of Mina and Van Helsing to the same place is steeped in the same atmosphere and Mina's stain marks her as one of the Devil's creatures. When Jonathan Harker reaches the castle and gradually discovers his host's real nature and meets the three she-vampires he is cut off from the rest of the world. Dracula lives in his castle, a true gothic fortress which soon proves to be a real Hell, for Jonathan is surrounded by living *'demons of the pit'* (38). Friendly Dracula is a fiend. Once he has left his country and castle, he spreads evil on the ship sailing to London, successively 'killing' the members of the crew. Dracula is a serial killer and London is his battlefield. London is the stage of the confrontation between the Crew of Light and the demon (of darkness) who first attacks and 'kills' Lucy before contaminating Mina. The weapons of the Crew of Light are the same that the peasants use in Transylvania, again mixing religion and superstition. It is only once Lucy has been destroyed completely and has received Arthur's *'mercy-bearing stake'* (216) that she becomes one of God's true dead, dead for good. The Crew of Light have done their duty but is there not an ambiguity in this merciful task? Lucy's death is performed through a desecration of her grave followed by a savage mutilation of her body, a rehearsal of the three she-vampires. The methods evoke the tortures of the Inquisition. A religion (etymologically the word means 'to bind, to link') that preaches love

seems to have turned into a parody of love, is even hatred. The only justification seems to be that the true dead are at peace at last but this is only the opinion of the good avengers, those narrators whose vision is lopsided and mediated through their own beliefs.

The Devil's Country

On his way to Transylvania when Jonathan tells the peasants about his destination, terror overwhelms them, all the more so as it is the eve of St George's Day: *'Do you not know that to-night, when the clock strikes midnight, all the evil things in the world will have full sway?* '(4). Vampires and witches were believed to be most active on the Eve of St George's Day.

The peasants come out with crucifixes, crossing themselves as if to ward off the devil. Superstition reigns supreme in the country to the extent that even rational Jonathan seems to be infected, he accepts the woman's crucifix despite his initial reluctance. Later on, when Mina and Van Helsing are pursuing Dracula, Mina declares, *'they are very very superstitious'* (361) as she feels she has to cover her forehead with a veil (an anagram of evil) to avoid suspicion. It is significant that the peasants should resort to weapons similar to those used by Van Helsing and his crew. Religion and superstition are closely intertwined. In his isolated Gothic castle, Dracula reigns supreme, like Satan in Hell, with his female vampires around him like Satan's imps. They keep Jonathan prisoner. It is a striking reversal of the Gothic pattern where it is usually the woman who is imprisoned. A number of critics have analysed the gender reversal that takes place in Dracula. Not only is Jonathan 'feminized' or infantilized but Dracula himself is both cook and housewife.

The book opens by toeing the Gothic line. In a faraway country, a helpless character is deceived into entering a dark castle of doom surrounded by sublime vistas of snowcapped mountains and some fathomless chasms. The maze is dramatised in a conventional way through the list, *'doors doors doors everywhere and all locked,'* or the melodramatic polyptoton and exclamation, '*the castle is a veritable prison and I'm a prisoner*!'(28) The helpless victim is male. In the magnificent derelict castle where the tapestries and curtains are more ancient than at Hampton Court, there is a touch of Beauty and the Beast in the way food and drink appear although there are no servants. The tale is fitted in two ways since this is stage-managed and the Count plays with both male and female roles. He is the bearded driver but also presumably Jonathan's cook and maid as he is seen making his bed, gendered anxiety is enhanced by unstable social roles (Lanone: 199-200).

Transylvania is the devil's country which Dracula fears leaving as he won't be accepted in England on the same terms, '*When I go there I shall be all alone*' (22). In the castle, Jonathan's fears increase and he uses the crucifix against the demons of the pit, which both repel and attract him:

> '*Two were dark and had high aquiline noses, like the Count's, and great dark, piercing eyes, that seemed to be almost red (…) The other was fair, as fair can be, with great, heavy masses of golden hair and eyes like pale sapphires. (…) I could feel the soft, shivering touch of the lips on the supersentitive skin of my throat, and the hard dents of two sharp teeth (…) I closed my eyes in a languorous ecstasy and waited—waited with beating heart*' (38).

Jonathan is under the empire of the vampire, the empire of the senses. Vampirism is sexual, hence reprehensible. These three Eves symbolize Evil and try to make vulnerable Jonathan fall. The scene of the assault upon Jonathan reverses the usual pattern of seduction. It is the women who try to penetrate Jonathan with the only instrument at their feminine disposal, their teeth ready to give him the fatal kiss, whereas Jonathan, turned Sleeping Beauty (the gender pattern is reversed, too), is waiting (im)patiently. The she-vampire is a Gothic-Romantic heritage (cf Keats's '*Lamia*' or Coleridge's '*Christabel*')

After his escape, Dracula embarks on a sea voyage where he starts his serial killing without any actual bloodletting. The voyage is the passage between Hell and Heaven, between the land of the devil and the land of God that will be contaminated by the devil on the ship. Dracula escapes from the ship in the form of a huge dog. Dracula will spread havoc over London, his polymorphism being another of his devilish weapons.

London, God's country and field of battle

Lucy is Dracula's first victim. The book could appear as an inverted Christian myth as Dracula takes blood instead of giving it. The world of vampires is a deformed Christian world, a black religion. To fight against Dracula, there is Van Helsing, another foreigner who, like Dracula, never has direct access to the narration, the good father figure who accepts the holy mission and prepares to defeat the devil with the help of his mates. Van Helsing and the four men are like Christ and his (more numerous) apostles. They resort to the same methods and use the same religious objects as the peasants in Transylvania: crucifixes, wafers, garlic, a mixture of religion and superstition as the enemy is the same. The banding together of the men smells of black magic: *'working together'*, *'we are pledged'*, *'solemn compact'*, *'in God's service'*, *'we are ministers of God's own wish'*. They feel endowed with a mission, to deliver the world from a polluting monster, to sterilize the earth, to prevent Mina from being forever banned from God. Dracula almost succeeds in perverting her.

Mina is vampirized (we'll stick to the euphemism) by the King. The reader witnesses it vicariously thanks to the men of the Crew of Light who keep insisting on the horror it provokes but who keep watching. Dracula both repels and fascinates. He reverses the usual roles as it is his own blood that is being drunk by Mina whom he forces upon an open wound in his breast in a frightful parody of a *madonna e bambino*, a Virgin Mary with a difference. This mother feeds her child whereas all the other she-vampires suck children's blood. In this initiation scene, Dracula compels Mina into the pleasure of vampiric appetite and introduces her to a world where gender distinctions collapse, where male and female bodily fluids intermingle terribly[1]. The scene is full of liquids and fluids—milk, blood and maybe something else, a symbolic act of enforced fellation and a lurid nursing.[2] When Mina relates the scene she baulks at a word she cannot bring herself to pronounce, and the word is replaced by a hyphen which paradoxically reinforces its strength by drawing the reader's ready attention, *'so that I must either suffocate or swallow some of the—Oh my God, my God'* (288). But God seems to be as mute and as powerless as a sleeping Jonathan. The whole scene, as the epitome of the whole novel, is a parody of a baptism or a wedding. (Bazin : unpublished article)

Van Helsing will actually later refer to it as a *'baptism of blood'* where water has turned to blood and Dracula has turned Mina into a monstrous daughter or a wife, *'flesh of my flesh'* (288), as if they were now one and the same in this incestuous unnatural union. It is Seward who describes this awful scene where Dracula, the *'demon-lover'* (the echo to *'Christabel'* is unmistakable), the erotico-exotic Don Juan like lover destroys the legitimate couples in a frightening reiteration that is also part and parcel of the fantastic genre. Dracula, the foreigner, takes the good men's wives in front of them without their moving an inch. Half comatose Jonathan is sleeping like a log or a baby while his wife is being vampirized by a very energetic virile Dracula. Van Helsing will later resume the idea, calling it a *'baptism of blood'* (322). It is both a perverted wedding and communion (drinking Christ's blood), the reverse of Mina and Jonathan's wedding which was a perfect example of true Christianity, devoid of any passion or sexuality. Dracula's wedding to Mina is as much of a parody as his killing of Lucy to whom he offers a cursed eternity. Eternal damnation is synonymous with unappeased lust and thirst for blood, animality. The descriptions of Dracula repeatedly stress the link with animals, especially wolves. He even turns into animals himself—bats, dog and rats. Dracula belongs to the heart of darkness as

---

1   Christopher Craft, 'Kiss Me with Those Red Lips' in 'Dracula', New Casebooks, ed. Glennis Byron, St Martin's Press, New York, 1999, p.110.

2   Ibid.

opposed to the Crew of Light. Daylight is fatal to him. The baptism of blood he has given Mina has infected her. The stigmata of the fatal kiss appears on her forehead, branded like Hawthorne's scarlet letter. Dracula's words sound retrospectively prophetic, *'flesh of my flesh'*. It will be the men's task to deliver her from evil, from the mark of sin. Mina herself, fearing her terrible end, asks for a burial service performed along the lines of perfect Christianity. Religion is both a safeguard and an incentive, giving the men the courage to go on with their duty in the service of God.

Gods or Demons?

It is in the name of religion that they act. If Dracula is the Devil (the name means devil in Romanian), he must be defeated by God's men to make Good triumph over Evil. If the aim appears noble, the means appear far less so. Lucy's true death is performed through the desecration of her grave and the savage mutilation of her body, which Van Helsing will reiterate with the three she-vampires at the end.

'*The Thing in the coffin writhed; and a hideous, blood-curdling screech came from the opened red lips. The body shook and quivered and twisted in wild contortions, the sharp white teeth champed together till the lips were cut and the mouth was smeared with a crimson foam. But Arthur never falted. He looked like a figure of Thor as his untrembling arm rose and fell, driving deeper and deeper the mercy-bearing stake*' (216)

The staking scene is one of the most heavily sexual scenes in the novel. Arthur, as a righter of wrongs is compared to the God Thor (of thunder and war), ready to 'dedemonize' Lucy, in a medieval or Shakespearian scene. Lucy's fiancé is thus cast as Othello, a man who perceives himself wronged by a passionate woman and consequently uses violence to reassert the patriarchal gender code.[3] Lucy, the witch, (one can play upon the double

---

3   Rebecca Pope, *'Writing and Biting in Dracula'*, in *'Dracula'*, New Casebooks, 68-92, 76.

meaning of 'stake') will be impaled as Vlad, Dracula's ancestor, used to impale his victims. It is up to Arthur to (s)take his wife in a scene where duty looks more like a sacrificial ritual or a crusade and becomes butcher-work. Arthur literally breaks his fiancé's heart, a surgical operation that aims at restoring order. It is, however, difficult to believe in the disinterestedness of their action. The men of the Crew of Light look more like wild beasts or Jacks the Rippers, thirsty for the blood of Lucy to whom, ironically, they have given so much of theirs. (Bazin: unpublished article)

What should be a work of love looks very much like a work of hatred. Mina has suffered more from Dracula's attacks than the four men in the Crew of Light yet she is the most ready to forgive, which reinforces the sustained imagery of Mina as Angel.

She is the Ruskinian epitome of tenderness, understanding, submission, self-sacrifice, finding her happiness only in making others happy, making duty her motto. She is the ideal idol, the light that Lucy, despite her name, has failed to embody.

The men on the other hand are like the soldiers of the Inquisition, frantically pursuing the enemy or its disciples. Their so-called holy mission is akin to barbarism. The staking is a masquerade of love-making but only the women are mutilated. If Dracula is a serial killer who turns his victims into so many others in his own image, the Crew of Light are frantic fanatical, killers, too, who take religion and morality as pretexts to perform their murders, violating the law. Their justification in giving death is also the fact that the true dead are at peace at last. *'There in the coffin lay no longer the foul Thing that we had so dreaded and grown to hate (...) but Lucy as we had seen her in her life, with her face of unequalled sweetness and purity'.* (216-217). A Sleeping Beauty who is asleep for good at last.

Eternal rest is substituted to eternal wandering. But can we trust so obviously biased narrators?

Religion appears as a reactionary ideology against foreigners, women, the oppressed. If the novel appears as religiously correct, it may not be politically so. The good are not as good as they seem, nor as dispassionate as they pretend to be. Christian duty wins in the end but at what cost! Civilized men have become savages in the name of God to perform their duty as they see it.

Under its religious aspect, *'Dracula'* is a phantasm, hence its mythical strength. It is the re-enactment of the Oedipal myth with Dracula as the father figure who wants to possess all the women and the jealous sons fighting against him, preferring to kill their women than to leave them to Dracula, Devil Daddy.

The interest of the novel is that, though it explicitly appears as a religious novel, it is also more than that, as the bulk of critical readings testifies—political, ideological, feminist criticisms, etc. The novel is as protean as Dracula himself, which no doubt accounts for its enduring success.

Bibliography

Bram Stoker, *'Dracula'* (1987), Oxford World's Classics, OUP, 1998. All references are to this edition.

'Dracula', New Casebooks, ed. Glennis Byron, St Martin's Press, New York, 1999.

Lanone, Catherine, *'Bram Stoker's Dracula or Femininity as a Forsaken Fairy-Tale in Dracula'*, Stoker/Coppola, ed. G. Menegaldo and D. Sipière, Ellipses, Paris, 2005, 199-209.

Bazin Claire, *'Women in Dracula'*, unpublished article.

'Dracula, L'œuvre de B. Stoker et le film de F.F. Coppola', eds. C. Bazin et S. Chauvin, Le Temps, Nantes, 2005.

THE SANEST MAN I EVER SAW

R. M. Renfield, aetat.59—'Sanguine temperament, great physical strength, morbidly excitable, periods of gloom, ending in some fixed idea which I cannot make out. I presume that the sanguine temperament itself and the disturbing influence end in a mentally-accomplished finish; a possibly dangerous man, probably dangerous if unselfish. In selfish men, caution is as secure an armour for their foes as for themselves. What I think of on this point is, when self is the fixed point the centripetal force is balanced with the centrifugal: When duty, a cause, etc., is the fixed point, the latter force is paramount, and only accident or a series of accidents can balance it'. (61)

Renfield, Seward's favourite patient, an inmate at the lunatic asylum overseen by Dr Seward, is first introduced by the Doctor in his diary (25th of April).

'I went down among the patients. I picked out one who has afforded me a study of much interest. He is so quaint in his ideas, and so unlike the normal lunatic, that I have determined to understand him as well as I can. Today I seemed to get nearer than ever before to the heart of his mystery' (60).

Seward is far, however, from having reached the end of his quest. Renfield's oxymoronic and hard-to-classify nature—'so *unlike the normal lunatic'*—may account for the difficulty in establishing a diagnosis. Labelling him a zoophagous patient is an attempt, on the part of Seward, at categorizing him in the hope of making his medical task easier. But Renfield escapes or defies any kind of categorization as he is subject to unforeseeable unpredictable changes. A lot of textual space is devoted to Renfield who, however, like Dracula, is never allowed direct access to the narration on account of his madness. Difference, be it racial (Dracula) or psychological (Renfield) is never on a par with the 'normality' of the good English men. As for Jonathan with Dracula, it will take the Doctor some time and many interviews with his favourite patient to guess that Renfield is a man *'under influence'* whose Master is no other than Dracula who savagely kills him in the end.

A medical case, *'not a normal lunatic'*.

'There is a method in Renfield's madness' (69), says Seward, linking him to one of his famous literary predecessors, *'And I like the flies; therefore I like it'* (116), a perfect example of syllogism. Renfield eats insects in a cumulative way, in the hope of obtaining their life-force, *'it was life, strong life, and gave life to him'* (69)—and will eat bigger and bigger ones, finally asking for a cat that would devour the birds that have swallowed the spiders that have killed the flies. When no longer able to control himself, unlike Dracula who managed not to suck Jonathan's bleeding throat, he even turns into a savage beast, *'he fought like a tiger'* (102); or a mad dog. *'He was lying on his belly on the floor licking up, like a dog, the blood which had fallen from my wounded wrist'* (141). The vampire who can control animals such as rats, bats and spiders has offered Renfield a Faustian pact. If Renfield worships him, he will provide him with an endless supply of food.

Like his Master, Renfield holds the belief that the more lives he absorbs, the stronger he will become. He imitates and echoes his Master Dracula, absorbing as much blood as he can or must. Not only does Renfield catch, he also keeps note of the number in a methodical way that evokes medical precision (69). Renfield is indeed a case oscillating between madness and calm, standing in an inbetween zone. *'The man is an undeveloped suicidal maniac'* (70) who fascinates Seward to the point that, Frankenstein-like, he yearns to have access to the workings of the brain to develop his own scientific research and experiments. If 'zoophagous' is a fitting label, it is, however, insufficient as Renfield is far more than that and escapes too restrictive a definition.

He is even capable of philosophical conversations about...

madness, '*Since I myself have been an inmate of a lunatic asylum, I cannot but notice that the sophistic tendencies of some of its inmates lean towards the errors of non causae and ignoratio elenchi*' (233), or science, '*The fly, my dear sir, has one striking feature: its wings are typical of the aerial powers of the psychic faculties. The ancients did well when they typified the soul as a butterfly*' (268), or again of behaving like a perfect gentleman with the men of the Crew of Light: '*He shook hands with each of them, saying in turn:—'Lord Godalming, I had the honour of seconding your father at the Windham;*' (243-44)—to the point that he baffles Seward himself, who is almost willing to believe that his reason has been restored (244) and that Quincey Morris even resumes and amplifies the initial oxymoron, '*he is about the sanest lunatic I ever saw*' (248). A lunatic who takes delight in playing with words in a poetic way: "*The bride-maidens rejoice the eyes that wait the coming of the bride; but when the bride draweth nigh, then the maidens shine not to the eyes that are filled.*' (101)[1]. A lunatic who has retained his sense of humour, '*They think I could hurt you! Fancy me hurting you! The fools!*' (107).

The anxiety of influence

Seward is not prepared to accept being puzzled by his patient who, as he repeats, is not a '*normal lunatic*' refusing to abide by the rules of the 'ordinary' mad. No wonder! Since Renfield obeys a power Seward is unaware of and even refuses to believe in at first. It will take Van Helsing's strong power of persuasion and his authority over his ex-pupil, together with the material evidence of Lucy's body, to convince incredulous rational Seward that Lucy is the prey of a vampire.

Throughout the novel, Seward tries to understand his patient's mysterious behaviour, repeating how difficult the task is, '*I wish I could get some glimpse of his mind*' (117) or, '*any clue of his thoughts*' (116) or again, '*I wish I could fathom his mind*' (116).

---

1   A spurious pseudo biblical speech with no real equivalent in the bible itself. Note in '*Dracula*', p.384

Though Seward is a psychiatrist, a brain specialist, he is at a loss: Renfield is both mad and wise, good and evil, as oxymoronic as Dracula himself.

During the course of the novel, Seward gradually guesses that he may be under the influence of Count Dracula, *'Strange that it never struck me that the very next house might be the Count's hiding-place!'* (225). When he baulks at the word 'drink', *'There isn't anything in them to eat or—'* (271), Seward has a kind of belated epiphany, *'Merciful God! The Count has been to him, and there is new scheme of terror afoot'* (272).

A number of passages are an illustration of Renfield's changing moods that seem to vary according to the time of the day, *'just before the stroke of noon'*, as if noon were a fatal, though 'unusual', time.

'For the first week after his attack he was perpetually violent. Then one night, just as the moon rose, he grew quiet, and kept murmuring to himself, 'Now I can wait, now I can wait.' (106-107).

Such outbursts are usually expected at midnight unless noon were *'the other side'* of midnight, as madness is the other side of reason. Right at noon, he becomes completely mad, so much so that it is difficult to hold him, for those who are used to it, which means that Renfield's crises tend to follow a repetitive pattern, which should make things easier. *'The attendant knew the symptoms.'* (115). But even if they are used to his outbursts, they are nonetheless surprised at their violence, the intensity of his screams that frighten all the other mad patients and even Seward himself. Screaming is a characteristic of madness where coherent language is defeated as with Bertha Rochester, the mad woman in the attic in Charlotte Brontë's, *'Jane Eyre'*. The screaming frightens all the other mad patients and even Seward himself. But his outbursts are quickly followed by suspiciously calm moods where he is sad and melancholy, not to say depressed, an attitude that has its cause in the 'Master's' departure or greater distance from him: *'He has deserted me'* (116), words which are a blasphemous echo to those of Christ's on the cross and which Seward is yet unable to understand. His address to a mysterious 'He' (the capital H indicating the importance of the addressee) is another mystery for Seward who—unlike the reader —cannot but wonder who 'He' is. 'He' is no other than Dracula, a mock God. The whole book could be read as a parody (of religion, of sex, of gender roles). Seward qualifies his voice as '*far away*', not of this world. Renfield sounds desperate and abandoned, all alone to accomplish his mysterious mission. His repeated and emphatic '*All over*' means that he believes nothing will ever bring Dracula back to him.

In such moments of depression, Renfield's moods are that of a sulking whimsical child to which Renfield is often compared, especially when he insists on getting what he wants, such as the much desired cat. He sits in a corner of the room, in the attitude of a child who has been punished. Like a child, too, he apologizes to the Doctor for having misbehaved even if this does not prevent him from going on with his captures, this time in a very happy mood putting the flies in a box-turned-coffin, keeping them prisoners. Seward waxes humorous in his description, '*a harvest of flies*' (115), as if he were paying Renfield a compliment for a good harmless job. He is also capable of violence: '*He fought like a tiger*' (102) or again, '*he had struck at me and cut my left wrist rather severely*' (141) or of repeatedly escaping the vigilance of his guardians, '*the patient has once more escaped*' (108), '*This time he had broken out through the window of his room*' (156).

What is puzzling about Renfield, and not only for Seward but also for the reader is that we never get any clear explanation as to Renfield 'meeting' with Dracula (the Coppola film gives an explanation, he has become mad after a stay at Dracula's castle). Renfield is not a vampire either. Dracula seems to prefer women's blood and he has obviously not drunk Renfield's although he has some vampiric attitudes derived from his strong belief in the power of blood, '*The blood is the life*' (141), which he absorbs but only indirectly in eating living animals. His physical strength is, however, to be compared with Dracula's although he will finally be defeated by the Master, ending in a pool of blood as if blood were his *'natural element'* or as if he were a sacrificial animal, an *'agnus dei'* or rather *'agnus diaboli'*.

A sacrificial victim

On meeting Mina Harker, the object of Dracula's obsession, Renfield, not unlike the other men in the novel, cannot but worship her and, knowing only too well the danger she is threatened with, he begs her to flee from his master. Renfield begs Seward and the others to allow him to leave lest he feel guilty for her fate, *'You will, I trust, Dr Seward, do me the justice to bear in mind, later on, that I did what I could to convince you tonight.'* (247). Desperately trying to save Mina by fighting Dracula, Renfield is finally defeated by the Master's hypnotic stare,

> *...'when she went away I began to think, and it made me mad to know that He had been taking the life out of her. I could feel that the rest quivered, as I did. (...)* 'So when He came to-night I was ready for Him. I saw the mist stealing in, and I grabbed it tight. I had heard that madmen have unnatural strength, and I knew I was a madman—at times anyhow—I resolved to use my power. Ay, and He felt it too, for He had come out of the mist to struggle with me. I held tight, and I thought I was going to win, for I didn't mean Him to take any more of her life, till I saw His eyes. They burned into me, and my strength became like water. He slipped through it, and when I tried to cling to Him, He raised me up and flung me down. There was a red cloud before me, and a noise like thunder, and the mist seemed to steal away under the door.'* (280)

When, later, vampire hunters enter the room Van Helsing manages to prolong Renfield's life for a while, which enables Renfield to tell his story to the vampire hunters who rush to help Mina and leave him lying on the floor. He dies shortly afterwards.

Conclusion

The text is an illustration of a peculiar case—zoophagous, mad, alternatively violent and calm, Renfield challenges medical knowledge. As a disciple of Dracula he cannot be easily classified, hence the fascination he holds for a specialist whose medical skills are inadequate because his case goes beyond them. Dracula is also a study in madness. Renfield's is never explained unless it be in terms of influence. He is a man under influence and he will die for it when Dracula deserts him totally and makes him pay for his protection of Mina. The blood may be the life but it is also the death.

DRACULA
AND POLITICS

JEAN-JACQUES LECERCLE

DRACULA AND POLITICS

1. The question of the relationship between *'Dracula'* and politics can be easily and immediately answered. Whereas *'Frankenstein'* is a progressive myth, *'Dracula'* is a reactionary myth. Not only in the non-pejorative sense of the term, in that, looking backwards to an ancient lineage, *'Dracula'* is a myth of ascendance, whereas *'Frankenstein'*, which looks forward towards the successors of the human race, a race of beings more agile and more intelligent than we are, is a myth of descendance. We may use the term 'reactionary', where *'Dracula'* is concerned, in the vulgar sense. *'Dracula'* is a reactionary novel because it is xenophobic, potentially racist, moved by a hatred of women that goes beyond the trivialities of typical Victorian male chauvinism. The question, then, becomes: how can we and how can I still find such a politically repulsive myth so fascinating? That question is in no way original except that my answer requires a deeper relationship between *'Dracula'* and politics.

2. The reactionary character of Dracula and the progressive character of Frankenstein can be demonstrated if we read the novel using the theoretical language of Alain Badiou's theory of the event. That is, through the cluster of concepts that structure his Being and Event. These are a situation, the language of the situation, the event that shatters the situation and entails definitive consequences—in the shape of affects and effects of truth, (the event creates a site of truth in the situation)—and of subjectivity (a militant subject emerges who will be the carrier of this truth). *'Frankenstein'* can be described as depicting such an event: the event of the apparition of man's successor as the king of creation, a new link in the great chain of being. The situation (Geneva at the end of the eighteenth century, with its social order, its customs, its family life and the language that expresses it all) is duly threatened with subversion. And a subject also appears to carry forth the truth of this event: the couple of Victor and the monster (in Badiou's theory, the subject

of truth is never an individual, not even the scientific genius that Victor is, but always a collective—here in its elementary form, the couple, as in love at first sight). The end of the tale, in the disappearance of this couple in the monster's suttee, is the result of the betrayal of the truth of the event by Victor, its initiator. For not all revolutions lead to *des lendemains qui chantent*.

In the case of *'Dracula'*, however, such a description is impossible. The novel is not the site of the emergence of the radically new but rather of the resurgence of the archaic, of a justly forgotten ancient past, of the always-already known (albeit repressed). The crux is, of course, the question of language. There is no language to express the radical novelty of the monster who is not even given a name. This is why Victor did not confide in the police: they would not have believed him; whereas the language in which the vampire can be named and, having been named, can be fought, is available in the tradition of which Van Helsing is the representative. This is why there are as many cloves of garlic as there are telegrams in *'Dracula'*, ancient superstition is not contradictory with current, even advanced, science—both are expressed in the language of the situation, pervaded with sedimented history. So, since the reappearance of the vampire does not lead society towards an exciting, if disquieting, future but threatens it with a return to the primeval social chaos, the question now becomes: if *'Dracula'* is not the site of an event, what is it the site of?

3. The answer involves a theoretical detour through the theory of delirium put forward by the Italian philosopher, Remo Bodei, in his book, *'Le logiche del delirio'*.[1] This theory of delirium takes as its point of departure a letter to Fliess, dated December 6th, 1896, in which Freud produces one of the first sketches of his psychological system, in what will become the expected form of a topography as in the tri-partition of ego, superego and id. Here, however, the topography has the form of a history, a chronology of the strata that make up the human psyche. The first stage, infancy, is the stage of bare perception with no memory and, consequently, no inscription

---

1   R. Bodei, *Le logiche del delirio: ragione, affetti, follia*, Bari: Laterza, 2002.

or 'registering' of the affects; the second stage, from 6 to 8 years, is the stage of perception with registering; the third stage, from 8 to 14 years, is the stratum of the constitution of the unconscious; the fourth stage, from 14 years onwards, is the stratum of the pre-conscious and the conscious. It is easy to understand why Freud never developed this sketch. It is flawed not least because it associates the unconscious with what is known as the latence period, chronology and topography do not go well together. Bodei, however, goes beyond such obvious aporia. He is interested in the introduction of the concept of repression. Freud explains that each stage has its own language, the language of the inscription of the events and affects that correspond to it. The language changes as the child goes from one stage to another. The events and affects of the former stage are re-transcribed in the new language. The name of such transcription is memory. But translation does not always work. There are episodes and affects that cannot be translated, that remain expressed in a now anachronistic language and as such are repressed. They derive their potentially painful characteristics from this failure of translation.

Here, Bodei uses the metaphor of the sea that has been mined by a hostile navy. Our psyche is such a sea in which concealed psychic mines are drifting. Sometimes one of them explodes causing a psychotic crisis that results in delirium (the number of such psychic mines varies with each individual). And we are only too aware of the existence of biological mines. One of their names is cancer. At this point, we must recognize that we have a non-trivial theory of delirium. The text of delirium is written in an archaic language, which has remained untranslated in the adult, conscious and rational stage. The question is: what has all this to do with '*Dracula*'?

My idea is that the vampire is the embodiment of one of those psychic mines. Even as, in Deleuze and Guattari, Plato's prisoner or the seducer according to Kirkegaard are '*conceptual characters*',[2] Count Dracula is a psychic character who embodies a feature of the human psyche. We begin to understand why the myth, however

---

2   G. Deleuze & F. Guattari, *What is Philosophy?*, London: Verso, 1994.

repulsive, is so fascinating. We all have a virtual Dracula at the back of our minds, in so far as we have repressed events and affects that belong to outmoded strata of our psychic constitution. The vampire crisis, which I once described as a crisis of witchcraft, is a psychic crisis:[3] These descriptions are not exclusive, if we remember J. Favret-Saada's account of witchcraft in the West Country of France.[4]

The question then becomes: if *'Dracula'* is the account of a psychic crisis, who is the subject of that crisis? Who, in the novel, is the lunatic? Renfield, of course, is a lunatic but he is not one of the major characters, even if the presence in the novel of a certified madman and his psychiatrist is a sign. The answer I would like to suggest is: not one character but two, the two women in the cast, Lucy and Mina (which explains, incidentally, why Dracula vampirises women only, why he spares Jonathan Harker who remains in his power for several weeks). The story of *'Dracula'* is the story of Lucy's incurable madness, of Mina's temporary insanity. It is the story of the deep-seated insanity of women, a Victorian theme, to which the etymology of the word 'hysteria' bears witness. Lucy founders on a psychic mine for the same reason that President Schreber, the famous patient of Freud, becomes mad. Success is too much for them. He has been appointed a high judge at an unusually tender age, she has reached the highest success a woman may aspire to: three proposals of marriage in one day! No wonder she immediately meets Dracula and becomes a vampire. And, incidentally, we also understand why, once the Count has drifted to Whitby and London, he is never heard to speak: psychic mines do not talk, they explode and they do not talk because theirs is an archaic unintelligible language repressed in the current state of the psyche.

---

3   J.J. Lecercle, 'The kitten's Nose: Dracula and Witchcraft', in F. Botting, ed., 'The Gothic', Cambridge: D.S. Brewer, 2001, pp. 71-86.

4   J. Favret-Saada, 'Les mots, la mort, les sorts', Paris: Gallimard, 1977.

4. My hypothesis, however, is based on an unacknowledged premise: women are particularly susceptible to encountering psychic mines, in other words they are prone to insanity or, which is the same thing, to falling under the spell of the vampire. This is a singularly misogynistic premise. It is also an integral part of the spontaneous ideology of the average Victorian and very much present in *'Dracula'* (hence, as I said, the vulgarly reactionary aspect of the novel). Purple passages abound. One might quote the passage in chapter eight in which Mina derides the New Woman like the feminine Uncle Tom that she is (*'Men are more tolerant, bless them'*). What is so dreadful about the New Woman is that she might like to do the proposing herself instead of waiting to be proposed to and that she might even want the prospective bride and bridegroom *'to see each other asleep'* before marriage—which constitutes an inversion of the sexual hierarchy in the matters of agency and freedom. Or again, one might quote the passage in chapter eleven where the keeper of the zoo, deploring the escape of his wolf, speaks with the *'wisdom of nations'* as we say in French, in the voice of solid common sense combined with the language of the true scions of the ancient British race, the lower classes, *'You can't trust wolves no more nor women.'* You will have noted, beyond the limited intelligence granted to women, their symbolic association with animals. Need I say more?

We are, of course, dealing with a distribution of character roles, that is with the literary representation of women in the Victorian novel. I have suggested elsewhere that the distribution of the women characters occurred around four actual and one virtual position, as in the following diagram:[5]

	2. Spinster	
1. Virgin	5. (Woman as subject)	3. Wife and Mother
	4. Whore	

5   J.J. Lecercle, 'The violence of style in 'Tess of the d'Urbervilles', in L. St John Butler, ed., *Alternative Hardy*, London: Macmillan, 1989, p. 8.

Lucy's progress but also Mina's may be charted on that diagram. Lucy goes from one to five, the excluded position and thence to four—she becomes a vampire because she is a vamp. Mina goes straight from one to three (five is not mentioned) and thence temporarily to four (when she is branded like a scarlet woman) but, protected by her passage in three, which has something definitive about it ('*till death them do part*'), she returns to that position and is delivered of the child, conceived in holy matrimony, that guarantees the happy ending of the tale.

5. One explanation of the virulent hatred of women that characterises the novel, if we forget for one moment the individual explanation, whether biographical or psychoanalytic and seek for a political, that is a collective, explanation, is that the novel was published in a conjuncture where male domination was under threat, both in practice ('*Dracula*' is, roughly speaking, a novel of the age of the suffragettes), in art ('*Dracula*' is a novel of the age of the New Woman novel—it was published in 1897, roughly at the same time as Menie Muriel Dowie's '*Gallia*') and in theory (Mill's '*The Subjection of Women*' was published in 1867 and Engels's '*Origin of the Family, Property and the State*', which reads like a feminist tract, was published in 1884). It would seem, then, that '*Dracula*' anticipates the post-68 feminist slogan, '*le personnel est politique*', although on the reactionary side of the divide. It is a political task of extreme urgency to teach women their place.

I think, however, that we can go beyond this blatant exhibition of reactionary political extremism. But, in order to do this, we need another theoretical detour. It starts with a question about the novel, why are the Crew of Light or in the more down to earth idiom of the second rate cowboy film, the 'goodies,' so numerous? In Proppian terms, the role of the hero subject of the quest is traditionally filled by a single character, be he the true knight or the lonesome cowboy, rather than by the sheriff's posse. The reason for this will become clear if we remember Freud's myth of the origins of society in '*Totem and Taboo*'. The gist of the myth can be phrased in a single sentence. Society takes its origin in communal murder. The murder is committed by the band of brothers, the victim is their father, an authoritarian patriarch with exclusive access to the women of the family or tribe. The myth, an extrapolation on the anthropological thinking of Freud's contemporaries, from Frazer to Robertson Smith, is part of an analysis of the concept of totem, of the sacrifice of the king or sacred beast, of the blood bond that the sacrifice creates among the faithful or the members of the clan. We note that in the Freudian myth the totemic father is not only murdered but eaten. The blood of the father is literally ingested by the cannibal sons. And we remember that this myth of the origin of society is also a myth of the origin of the family. For Freud, the family is the modern equivalent of the archaic primitive horde in which the father has recovered part of the power he had lost to his sons— a compromise formation between the father's authority and the sons' newly gained rights.

I am not the first to note how close this myth is to Dracula. The vampire is the archetypal figure of the jealous father who lays claim to all the women (we understand why the Count vampirises only women), who must be killed not by the solitary hero but by the associated brothers and who cannot be killed anywhere but only in his own home. Of course, in '*Dracula*' the associated brothers are not cannibals. It is the vampire who drinks blood, but the displacement is easy to understand. We remember that in the novel most of the heroes give their blood to save Lucy who is, therefore, described as '*a sweet polyandrist*'—she it is who embodies the blood bond between the heroes. And we understand why the vampirising of women by Dracula has such explicit sexual connotations, why it is always described as a form of rape. We understand why the totemic vampire, and he only, is associated with an animal and why the Count is so old. Not because he has survived himself as a vampire but because he is the archaic father, the father of society and the family—the embodiment of a myth, if origin is quite fittingly as old as Methuselah.

But I believe this also goes a long way towards explaining what I may now call the Freudian fascination for the repulsive reactionary myth. The guilt of the original murder does not haunt only the first generation of criminals but all their descendants as well. In a sense, Dracula is the myth of the terrifying return of the archaic father who comes back to exert his revenge, a more cruel and vindictive version of the ghost of Hamlet's father. No wonder such a powerful myth still strikes a chord in us.

6. So '*Dracula*' has a more general relation to politics. It is a political myth in the widest sense, in that it is a myth of the origins of the polis, of the city. What is re-played in the novel is the threat to society and family that the authoritarian patriarch represents and the re-foundation of the city by his violent elimination. And it is a reactionary myth in a wider sense, in that it is based on the violence of parricide, and, therefore, carries with it a conception of human nature as inherently violent. Not all myths of origin are reactionary in this sense. We may quote the myth of primitive communism in Marx and Engels or the myth of the origin of society in Aristotle (man is a political animal in so far as he is a talking animal). So I think I should reconsider the violence that the myth inscribes.

There is one possible objection to my reading of '*Dracula*' by way of '*Totem and Taboo*'. The most violent scene of rape is not committed by Dracula but by the Crew Of Light when they kill Lucy, the female vampire, in a scene which can only be described as a collective rape, what is vulgarly known as a gang bang. The scene is narrated by Dr Seward (who had proposed to Lucy) and I am struck by the intensity of the sadistic hatred he expresses, which goes far beyond the natural effect of the disappointed lover. '*At that moment the remnant of my love passed into hate and loathing; had she to be killed, I could have done it with savage delight.*' No wonder if at the end of the scene he compares Lucy to Medusa. I spare you the Freudian analysis of the myth of Medusa with her snakes and pointed teeth except to remind you that Freud ascribes an apotropaic function to the mythical character of the castrating woman.

It would appear that the victim of the associated brothers' rage is not only the tyrannical father but the woman, always-already caught in a state of adultery. In other words, what the perennial myth (Bram Stoker, talibans, même combat) represents through its inveterate hatred of women is the origin of all the forms of domination and exploitation in the domination and exploitation of one gender by the other, of women by men. This is why such a repulsive myth survives through all historical conjunctures, why it has not lost its power of fascination: because it is in its reactionary form, that is in the form of the illusion produced by hatred. It says the truth about the origin of society, not the pessimistic truth envisaged by Freud, which is predicated on a dubious conception of human nature but the more palatable truth inscribed in Engels's account of the origin of the family—not in brutal patriarchy but in the paradisiacal matriarchy of primitive communism. For Engels, as we know, the history of humankind before it became the history of the class struggle was the story of the exploitation of women by men—women are the original proletariat.

It is pretty clear on which side of this divide Dracula is situated. The vampire anticipates the Freudian patriarch because Freud's myth is hardly more than an exploitation of the dominant conception of the relation between the sexes. All he does is transform the thickest common sense into what Althusser calls *a spontaneous philosophy for scientists.*[6] The history of the vampire is an intervention within a historical and political conjuncture. We understand why the female vampire is put to death through collective rape and gruesome lynching (*'the Professor and I sawed the top of the stake, leaving the point of it in the body. Then we cut off the head and filled the mouth with garlic'*—such desecration of the body is still for us the sign of the utmost violence). She is the incarnation of women's revolt against male domination and as such must be made an example of, like Spartacus the slave leader and the leaders of the peasant rebellion in medieval Germany. The intensity of the effect of hatred is a symptom of the fear that the possible ending of male domination inspires in certain men—not the progressive type.

---

6   L. Althusser, *'Philosophy and the Spontaneous Philosophy of the Scientists'*, London: New Left Books, 1971.

I once described Frankenstein's monster as a *sans culotte*, a French revolutionary out to hang the aristocrats:[7] in Lucy, we must perceive the march of the New Woman, the incipient suffragette. The tale of *'Dracula'* does have a central relation to politics. And as the political questions it seeks to address are addressed in the form of fantasy, I think we can understand both our repulsion (as the myth does not offer the right solutions) and our fascination (such solutions have existed throughout history yet these questions still need to be discussed realistically).

But the explanation of the fascination the myth undoubtedly exerts is still a little thin. Let us go one step further and sum up the argument.

If a reactionary myth can also be a fascinating and persistent myth, it is because our political unconscious, to speak like Jameson,[8] is always threatened by a psychic mine, which survives the demise of all historical conjunctures: that mine may be called fear of the other, a rich source of hating and hateful affects. The name of the object changes—the leper, the Jew, the communist, the bogus asylum seeker, to quote Tony Blair, the gay or lesbian, the Muslim or any member of an ethnic minority and always women. We are all threatened by fits of racism, xenophobia, misogyny, and it requires a constant struggle in the political and social arena, but also in our very heads, to get rid of it. The psychic mine is always ready to blow up, the repressed archaic affect to return. And this return of the political repressed is as dangerous in our conjuncture as in Dracula's London. You can even become the President of the French Republic (albeit for one term only) by a careful exploitation of psychic mines.

We now fully understand both the persistence of the myth (all history is the history of the struggle against the other or of the fear of the other) and its fascination for us who in no way condone the reactionary ideology the text proudly disseminates. *'Dracula'*, for us, has indeed apotropaic value. By focusing on the archaic fear of the other which we like everyone else feel, in a context where it becomes

---

7   J.J. Lecercle, *'Frankenstein, mythe et philosophie'*, Paris: PUF, 1988.

8   F. Jameson, *'The Political Unconscious'*, London: Routledge, 1981.

caricatured, the myth may help us to master it and vanquish it: the mine does blow up but at a safe distance from our hull.

And we also, finally, understand the function of the fantastic as a literary genre (it is an apotropaic genre) and its division into two sub-genres, the fantastic of the event where anxiety towards the radically new is expressed as in '*Frankenstein*' and the fantastic of the psychic mine where our constitutive fear of and adherence to the archaic is expressed as in '*Dracula*'. What we learn from '*Dracula*' is that fantasy can be, must be, political.

TEXT CIRCULATION: THE BIRTH OF A NEW METAPHOR

SAMIA OUNOUGHI

TEXT CIRCULATION: THE BIRTH OF A NEW METAPHOR

What if Dracula had won the battle against Mina's team? Dracula's bites turn his victims into vampires who then forever crave for blood just like him. If the process of vampirism were to be taken to its final stage, *'Dracula'* would be an eschatological book, an apocalyptic novel, for the world would then be peopled with vampires, and there would simply be nothing left of human kind. Nothing would be left of vampires either, since they would have no fuel left to remain un-dead. The end of the story would have sounded the bell of the end of history. Dracula loses either way because vampirism is sterile, it is a dead end. This is different from his opponents who cultivate fertile text, people who read text, write and edit. Being un-dead means not being dead but it also implies not belonging to the living either, which also defines vampirism as sterile. Dracula's case is a negative definition of what existing means. What comes to an end when someone becomes a vampire is their participation in the circle of life, a circulatory system in which each individual is a link in a chain from which they get the necessary ingredients to be alive while supplying the other links of the chain with their own material. In *'Dracula'*, the circulation system on which life depends is the circulation of blood between individuals. Life also depends on text circulation through reading, writing and book editing. In this article, I will show how these two circulation systems are merged in the novel to give birth to a new metaphor.

Previous research works on *'Dracula'* have mainly focused on either the sexual aspect of the novel or on its complex and challenging narrative structure. Articles and books in the field of gender studies, psychoanalysis or socio economics have revealed the former aspect of Stoker's text while the later was explored through narrative discourse analysis. There are few examples in which both the sexual and textual aspects have been studied together as two faces of the same coin. Among the few that do both, Jennifer Wicke[1] solves the paradox of the blood and text aspects by showing that a Marxist approach and a psychoanalytical one are eventually not alien but complementary provided modern sexuality is seen as consumption. Blood and text are also studied together in *'Black and White and Read All Over: Performative Textuality in Bram Stoker's Dracula'*. Here, Harriet Hustis looks at the text from the recipient's point of view, using Wolfgang Iser's theories to state that performative textuality results from the act of reading which triggers the dynamic interplay between the figurative (Mina) and the imaginary (Count Dracula).

Here, I will show that Bram Stoker's *'Dracula'* brings forward the modern idea that human kind depends on the business of book publishing as much as blood circulation between people. First, I will demonstrate how the elements in Stoker's time made blood circulation a metaphor of text circulation. Then, I will examine the case of the vampire to explain how the process of vampirism detaches vampires from life as a circulation system. Finally, looking at the character of Mina Harker, I shall analyse how the writer develops his status to that of editor and explain the major role of the editor in the text circulation system.

Medical progress:
Dracula loses the privilege of blood transfusion

The emergence of the new metaphor, that of blood circulation as an image of text circulation, was partly rendered possible by the progress of medicine and partly by that of the book publishing industry in Stoker's time. In *'La Métaphore vive'*, Paul Ricoeur writes,

---

1   Wicke, Jennifer. *'Typewriting: Dracula and Its Media'* in ELH, Vol 59, N°2 (Summer, 1992), pp. 467-493. The John Hopkins University Press.

'Max Black's comparison between model and metaphor, [...] between an epistemological concept and a poetic one, will allow us to thoroughly exploit this idea which directly opposes all reduction of metaphor to a mere 'ornament'.

If we examine closely this suggestion, metaphor must be said to hold information for it *'re-describes' reality'*.[2] Indeed, something happened around the time *'Dracula'* was published. Both publishing and blood transfusion would now be vital to the needs of mankind. The histories of book publishing and blood transfusion would, from this point, be much closer. This new parallel was to give a new meaning to the vampire legend. In order to sense how the two notions of blood and text circulation are intermingled, metaphor should not be understood as a syntagm or as a sentence but as a whole complex system as Ricoeur further explains,

'First the model's exact counterpart, on the poetic side, is not exactly what we have called the metaphoric utterance, that is to say a brief speech which is most of the time limited to a sentence; the model rather consists of a complex network of utterances, its exact counterpart therefore being the continued metaphor—the fable, the allegory [...]'.[3]

The Count's means to supply himself with blood and the choice of his victims actually synthesises the history of blood transfusion. From the fifteenth century when the first attempt of blood transfusion was carried out, to the turn of the twentieth century, when medical progress led to successful blood transfusions, the blood circulation system was limited to each individual's body. The only way to pass blood from one individual to another was hereditary hence the many rich and enlightening

---

2   'Le rapprochement opéré par Max Black entre modèle et métaphore, autrement dit entre un concept épistémologique et un concept poétique, nous permettra d'exploiter à fond cette idée qui va directement à l'encontre de toute réduction de la métaphore à un simple «ornement». Si l'on va jusqu'au bout de cette suggestion, il faut dire que la métaphore porte une information, parce qu'elle 're-décrit' la réalité.» (Ricoeur: 32)

3   'D'abord le répondant exact du modèle, du côté poétique, n'est pas exactement ce que nous avons appelé l'énoncé métaphorique, c'est-à-dire un discours bref réduit le plus souvent à une phrase; le modèle consiste plutôt en un réseau complexe d'énoncés; son vis-à-vis exact serait donc la métaphore continuée la fable, l'allégorie [...] » (Ricoeur: 306).

Freudian sex/blood comparative analyses of *'Dracula'*. Dracula's crimes throughout the novel retrace the history of these failed experiments of blood transfusion through centuries, which already foreshadows the looming end of the vampire. Indeed, medical and chemical advancement as well as the spreading and improving level of education among the masses would soon render Dracula's self-providing-blood method completely outdated. In *'The Narrative Method of Dracula'*, David Seed highlights the vampire's fall from the status of the monster that inspires fear to that of a marginal creature whom humans can study and understand.

'The less Dracula is formulated, the more of a threat he represents. Once the different accounts have been put together, Dracula begins to diminish in stature. He turns out to be subject to Nature's laws (though only some of them) and to be a disappointingly conventional embodiment of Nordau's and Lombroso's criminal type.' (Seed: 74).

Back in the fifteenth century, the first attempt of blood transfusion from three boys to a Pope resulted in the deaths of the four participants[4]. The reason for this was that the Pope was given the boys' blood to drink. Just like Dracula, he took the blood into his mouth. At that time, scientists did not yet know that our digestive and blood systems were different. In fact, since Antiquity, when the Greeks believed that our blood and digestive systems were one, little progress had been made in centuries. Blood was also believed to convey character and thoughts (Argoud: 144). Dracula again mirrors these ancient and false beliefs as he acquires his victims' thoughts and knowledge once he has taken their blood. Yet, during the scientific revolution of the nineteenth century, progress speeded up dramatically which precipitated the end of the fear of vampires, especially because humans were soon to be safely transfused blood, too. In Stoker's days, it was, therefore, urgent that Dracula should now be confined to a tale, forever his only proper place.

---

4   Not all Historians agree on this anecdote, as they could not verify it with certainty.

Two centuries after the first attempts to transfuse blood experiments between humans and animals, the same experiments were performed again, the former providing blood for the latter. These attempts also resulted in fatal issues. While British physician, William Harvey, had successfully transfused blood from one animal to another all the attempts to transfuse blood into a man's body remained fatal[5]. Here again, Count Dracula's refilling his blood vessels with either animals' or humans' blood was already outdated in Stoker's time. It was in the late 1810s that Blundell discovered that blood transfusions should only be performed between humans (Starr: 35). Bram Stoker's book is not only modern, it anticipates a very near future because, when it was published, the evolution of medical sciences rendered the circulation of blood, our fluid of life, possible between humans.

Blood transfusion, which was then successful only in about 50% of the cases (Starr: 37), was soon to replace bleeding which gradually proved to be lethal rather than curing (Starr: 28). The opposition between pure blood (when it is red and within the body) and impure blood (when it is black and outside the body: Argoud: 136) proved invalid because blood effusion ceased to be lethal. Blood effusion could even save lives provided blood was properly channelled from one body to another. Only four years after the publication of 'Dracula', Landsteiner discovered the difference between human blood groups (Star: 38-39) and with the apparatus earlier developed to prevent blood clotting (Starr: 30-49) blood transfusion ceased to be a danger. The success of such a process meant that from then blood circulation would no more be limited to the intimacy of a body. It could be passed on from one human to another. As Stoker's novel shows by the various transfusions completed on Lucy, blood reception ceases to be vampires' privilege. Besides, Dracula's transfusion method proves to be completely wrong, which people will soon discover thanks to text circulation. Noble as he may be, Count Dracula loses the privilege of refilling his veins with blood, but he also forfeits being a well-read creature.

5   Starr, Douglas. Blood, 'An Epic History of Medicine and Commerce'. Little, Brown and Company, London, 1998. (3-15)

Progress in publishing:
Dracula loses the privilege of reading

Before the end of the nineteenth century, book publishing became a go-getting business. Besides blood circulation, the circulation of books contributed in tying links between humans thus rendering them a stronger species. This is not to say that the publishing business was born in Bram Stoker's time. But the Industrial Revolution as well as the increase of the literacy rate rendered the circulation of books easier and wider among the British population. The book industry flourished in Britain and in the British Empire (Weedon: 31-32). About 90% of the population of England and Wales could read by the end of the century when only half could fifty years before (Weedon: 51). If they could not all purchase books, the majority could borrow them (Weedon: 33). Book hunger increased in the 1880s and 90s, which allowed publishers, now equipped with the powered press, to increase their production massively if a book sold well and to charge a price low enough for the most modest classes to buy it. (Weedon: 159). 'Dracula' is a modern novel that illustrates its age. It inaugurates the birth of a new metaphor that pictures blood circulation and text circulation as mirror systems. Just as with blood circulation, book circulation has become a vital source of strength accessible to many more people. This is the very sign of Dracula's end.

When Jonathan visits Count Dracula the vampire has been un-dead for more than four centuries. Since he became a vampire, he has lost his place in the circle of the living. Nonetheless, he needs not to die. His struggle to keep this half-way position between the living and the dead is rendered manifest by the way he nourishes his body to stay alive and by the way he keeps his general knowledge and mastery of language to communicate with humans and eventually keep his power over them.

On arriving at Dracula's castle, Jonathan Harker is struck by the peculiar character he meets in the person of the Count. Harker notes what exotic or notable features he finds there. He remarks that Dracula possesses a vast library and that he is extraordinarily well-read: *'In the library I found, to my great delight, a vast number of English books, whole shelves full of them, and bound volumes of magazines and newspapers.'* (30). The many books he has in his library are signs of the Count's wealth and of his privilege to read much and build knowledge. Dracula is now in a world that he cannot conquer without knowing it and this implies being well read.

'These companions,' and he laid his hand on some of the books, 'have been good friends to me, and for some years past, ever since I had the idea of going to London, have given me many, many hours of pleasure.' (31).

This part of the narrative is described through Jonathan's eyes while he is still unaware that Dracula has been a vampire for centuries. In fact, impressive as it may be, Dracula's knowledge, especially in history, is the result of over four centuries of personal experience. Dracula's ambition to conquer a country in the modern world renders reading necessary, for he has to know his victims' language and context to impose his power over them.

But the mass of publication is increasing so Dracula is having more and more difficulties in keeping himself informed. The presence of periodicals in his library is an indicator of the accelerating flow of texts he has to read, *'A table in the centre was littered with English magazines and newspapers, though none of them were of very recent date.'* (30). This is confirmed by Mina's scrupulous edition process. The articles that she reads in the newspapers she gives a longer lasting form by storing them as clippings in her diary. *'Cutting from 'the Dailygraph,' 8 August (pasted in Mina Murray's Journal)'* (95). Meanwhile, Dracula is reading texts that have a less permanent form (literally, periodicals) and has or takes no time to store them. It reveals that reading, which along with blood consumption was one of his major strengths, is becoming his weakness because he has more and more competitors in the race to access knowledge for power.

Other characters in the novel are also well-read. Among them, the only aristocrat is Lord Godalming. Dr. Seward and Professor Van Helsing are experts in medicine and they keep researching. Yet the most striking cases are those of Jonathan and Mina. They are of modest lineage and they don't have so prestigious a job as MDs. Yet, the clerk and the training secretary will be Dracula's most powerful enemies since their job is not only to read but also to write and order texts. Both of them are curious and endowed with a talent for observation of their environment and of texts. Mina, in particular, is a brilliant text analyser and learns much more from her readings than anyone else in the novel. She is a reader of the paradigm. Not only does she read stories, she tries to get the meaning of them by constructing various networks of meaning regardless of the chronology of events or of their syntagm as her memorandum shows (417-419). She is even the bearer of the very modern idea that the reader may get more from the text than its author himself, paying minute attention to style. '*I think that the cylinders which you gave me contained more than you intended me to know. But I can see that there are in your record many lights to this dark mystery.*' (266). She understands along with Professor Van Helsing that the textual medium can reveal more than a discussion with the author and that there is more to a text than a mass of information. Finally, Jonathan and Mina can read more than one set of signs as they can decipher shorthand, which emphasizes their superiority over Dracula. Being more numerous and more skilled in deciphering and analysing, Dracula's modest enemies represent a new generation of learned and learning people, which is undoing Dracula's power as he is losing the social and cognitive monopoly of self-cultivation.

Besides, Dracula is selfish and keeps his knowledge to himself. The whole process of vampirism including blood consumption and reading now proves to be sterile. Among Dracula's victims for instance, Renfield and Lucy are no more learned once Dracula has bitten them. He ingests their thoughts and knowledge but transmits nothing to them. This self-centered attitude is going to weaken him, too. Meanwhile, Mina breaks the seal of her husband's journal thus throwing the first beam of light on the Dracula mystery. She continues the process with Professor Van Helsing by demanding that each member of the team read all the texts they can gather. Not one brain but a network of brains is now working on the same texts, shedding complementary lights on the evil that threatens to terminate them. Dracula is conscious that bearing knowledge is a source of power, what he ignores is that sharing knowledge exponentially increases strength. That is when text circulation becomes vital and Mina will set the conditions necessary to launch and spread this circulation.

'No one need ever know, shall ever know,' I said in a low voice. She laid her hand on mine and said very gravely, 'Ah, but they must!'

'Must! But why?' I asked.

'Because it is a part of the terrible story, a part of poor Lucy's death and all that led to it. Because in the struggle which we have before us to rid the earth of this terrible monster we must have all the knowledge and all the help which we can get'. (266)

Nourishing blood, nourishing text

Before analysing Mina's job as an editor, we need to inquire further into the parallel between blood and text. Having blood in our veins is vital. Nevertheless, if this blood is not provided with nourishment, it is useless. Blood conveys energy. To phrase this more appropriately here, it conveys power but it does not generate it. That's the major difference between humans and vampires.

As a future victim, Jonathan is welcomed with a solid dinner at Dracula Castle. Here, he notes that Dracula himself does not eat and later notes his surprise at never seeing the Count eat. *'It is strange that as yet I have not seen the Count eat or drink.'* (38). Dracula's body is deprived of a digestive system. That, too, defines him as undead. It means that he can take nothing from his environment but blood for survival. He has simply lost the capacity to transform food into energy. The power he gets must, therefore, come from others who still have this capacity. Once the energy contained in his victims' blood has been drained, their blood becomes useless to him as it has no more power to convey. Therefore, the very nature of blood is transformed. As soon as it is ingested by a vampire, blood ceases to be the fluid of life and becomes a mere fuel for life instead. In this respect, vampires can be compared with modern apparatus. They are like mobile phones with batteries but no charger to refill them with power.

On the contrary, humans do have a digestive system. The team that fight Dracula are thus often represented eating solid meals. Professor Van Helsing and Mina insist that they should all eat much. Mina says: *'Breakfast is ready, and we must all eat that we may be strong.'* (352). Van Helsing twice gives the men an order to eat much when Lucy needs blood:

'Now take down our brave young lover, give him of the port wine, and let him lie down a while. He must then go home and rest, sleep much and eat much, that he may be recruited of what he has so given to his love.' (150).

Later, he says again, *'Now you go home, and eat much and drink enough. Make yourself strong.'* (158). They all belong to the circle of life as they have this capacity to transform matter into power. Consequently, blood transfusion is for them only a specific need in extreme cases but on a daily basis their own blood remains rich and keeps them alive. Blood in their body remains the fluid that conveys the fuel their body is capable of transforming.

This transformation of one's natural environment into power that animates humans ('animate' must here be understood both as 'breathing' and 'soul' following its Latin root 'anima') works exactly the same when it comes to text production. All the texts that compose *'Dracula'* convey information in the form of speech representations resulting from sensorial perception. This is exactly the way in which cognitive linguists as Lakoff define metaphor. These texts are journals, letters or newspaper articles. The characters that write them feel the need, specific to human nature, to represent, that is to transform what they experience into speech. Jonathan, for instance, senses the vital task he is completing in writing a detailed account of his experience in Transylvania.

'I began to fear as I wrote in this book that I was getting too diffuse. But now I am glad that I went into detail from the first, for there is something so strange about this place and all in it that I cannot but feel uneasy.' (37).

By formulating their representation of the world, they convert perception into knowledge that they thus breed. This capacity to generate knowledge through perception and representation is the privilege of humans and this is precisely what Dracula lacks.

Dracula writes nothing. He breeds no knowledge and is therefore sterile as he has lost his capacity to generate any representation. His own image does not even appear in a mirror anymore. He literally has no more power of reflection. The latter argument could easily be countered as Jonathan receives two notes from the Count and has communicated with his solicitor in England. Yet, no narrative passage describes him putting his quill to paper himself. The only occasion on which he expresses the need to write is when he threatens Jonathan to do it for him. Even then, Dracula's letters are not efficient as he cannot make Jonathan's speech his own. On reading these letters, though handwritten and signed by Jonathan, Mina cannot possibly identify her fiancé in this speech and senses the strangeness of both their contents and style: 'It is only a line dated from Castle Dracula, and says that he is just starting for home. That is not like Jonathan. I do not understand it, and it makes me uneasy.' (91). Dracula needs people who can write instead of him, which is a clerk's (Jonathan) or a secretary's (Mina) job. These two characters are precious to him, hence his sparing of their lives several times. Yet, what he needs from them he cannot take, for he cannot appropriate their speech. This incapacity to have a speech of his own implies that he has no power of representation, no power of breeding metaphors that is his own vision of the world through which he could impose his power. Again, the bell rings that announces his end, for Dracula is now facing a new world into which many more people, be they as modest as a clerk, can decide to convey their own voice through text. Dracula now has to cope in a world in which even a woman can edit a book of her own.

Humans' capacity to generate knowledge, to give a representation of their experience, is only efficient if they rightly measure the vital function of text circulation. Lucy, for instance, fails to understand the far-reaching importance of text production. She is merely another, if delicious, meal for Dracula. It doesn't matter that much if she dies as she is no metaphor breeder. Yes, Lucy writes but her letters are full of paralipses *'I have nothing to tell you. There is really nothing to interest you.'* (71), for she has nothing to say. Mina even reproaches her with not writing enough: *'Tell me all the news when you write. You have not told me anything for a long time. I hear rumours, and especially of a tall, handsome, curly-haired man??? '* (71). She only writes more when she is proposed to by three men because Mina has urged her to give her a detailed account of her life and she is the one who gives her the subject of the letter about her love life. In this, Lucy proves no better than the vampire himself. Then she decides to write an account of her days but it is too late. Moreover, she does not even seize the reason why she is doing it, she only mimics Mina in this, *'I must imitate Mina, and keep writing things down.'* (133). Wanting to be someone else, taking after someone else, is another of Lucy's traits which brings her closer to the vampire species than to her own. Unconscious of her body and above all of her mind, Lucy is the perfect victim for Dracula.

As for Dr Seward, Jonathan and Arthur, they write but they do not perceive the crucial need to take their work a step further by ushering their texts into a circulation system. Seward starts recording his observations of Renfield to heal his broken heart and he does not want anyone to listen to his account of Lucy's death on his phonograph: *'No! No! No! For all the world. I wouldn't let you know that terrible story!'* (264). Jonathan writes whatever appears strange to him and later gives himself his own texts for company and witnesses not to die a madman. Though he allows Mina to read his journal, he does not want her to give him comments about her reading thus hindering text circulation.

> *'Here is the book. Take it and keep it, read it if you will, but never let me know unless, indeed, some solemn duty should come upon me to go back to the bitter hours, asleep or awake, sane or mad.'* (129).

On the contrary, Mina, along with Van Helsing, insists that each member of the team must thoroughly read whatever the other parties have written.

In wanting to perfect her skills as a secretary, Mina perhaps first appears as the perfect wife in her husband's shadow. Her personal endeavour to work on existing texts as well as her own and to give them their final shape, however, reveals how bright she is in understanding the importance of editing a text so that it can reach the greatest number of readers. By working to set the conditions necessary to put the text into circulation, she becomes an editor with the power to terminate Dracula, thanks to knowledge. She weakens him by narrowing the gap between the pieces of information about him that each member of her team brings. In doing so, Dracula, who is a question and a source of fear at the beginning, is gradually converted into a fully and logically describable object. As the all-mighty editor, she forces the vampire to be represented in the way that she chooses.

Indeed, if Mina can take the job, it is because she is multi-skilled. She can read, write, gather and shape the papers she requests into a powerful book. She can also read shorthand and operate a phonograph. Her charm and speech inspire trust and she, therefore, accesses all the recordings easily. Once she has these texts in her possession, she applies the conditions that will endure in the text circulation system. To terminate Dracula, the greatest number of people should know about him. Mina, therefore, converts shorthand texts into plain English. She renders the recordings on the phonograph more accessible by typewriting their contents. She renders the medium more permanent by typewriting several copies of the texts and by keeping the newspaper articles within her diary.

Once the texts are converted into a more permanent and readable form, the whole bulk must be given a narrative structure. Beyond this point, we are not informed whether the choices were made by Mina or not. Whoever decides what form the text should take to reach as many readers as possible must arrange the order of the documents so that the final text seduces the recipients. The text must be made thrilling and the order into which the fragments fall together is crucial. For instance, some parts of Mina's diary are not published in chronological order and her diary is cut in the midst of the same entry. For instance, Dr Seward wrote an entry in his diary on November 2. Only then does, Mina's entry written on October 31 appear.

Mina also keeps the privilege of access to speech,

> 'But I have been more touched than I can say by your grief. That is a wonderful machine, but it is cruelly true. It told me, in its very tones, the anguish of your heart. It was like a soul crying out to Almighty God. No one must hear them spoken ever again! See, I have tried to be useful. I have copied out the words on my typewriter, and none other need now hear your heart beat, as I did.' (266)

In saying this, Mina also keeps the privilege of access to direct speech and transforms Seward's voice into a typewritten text. This means she is the master of the final text. She brings forward the idea that representation in writing renders speech less sensational but further reaching, less individual and more universal as it becomes a pure medium of knowledge transmission.

Seduction is how Dracula recruits his victims. Poetics is the type of seduction that will defeat him. Dracula is a seducer but the action of his charm appears as a dive into shallow water when compared with the mastery of both poetics and text circulation possessed by the editor.

Mina The Modern Editor

Mina ends Dracula by ushering him into the circle of life by turning him into a book that describes him through the eyes of those who have had to struggle against him. In this respect, she represents the modern woman who is not limited to giving birth to children. She can also train and cultivate her mind and set up a book project and manage it. She knows that text must be put into a condition of reproduction so it can be regenerated by the process of reading which itself would not happen without printed books. Mina is a modern editor even to the present day reader. Her questions apply well to our current global society in which the development of diverse and fast evolving modes of publication threatens the long-lastingness of our text productions. This is why she types the recorded accounts on Dr Seward's phonograph. Indeed, it was in Stoker's time a very modern tool but Mina realizes that it can in no way challenge the book format as it is not widely spread, not easily transportable and difficult to re-examine to find passages. Thanks to Mina's work, '*Dracula*' now belongs to mainstream culture.

Stoker wrote his book at a seminal moment. Medical progress gave people the means to share their blood. The improvements in the educational system along with the expansion of the publishing industry gave people the means to acquire more knowledge. This gave birth to a new metaphor, which '*Dracula*' incarnates. At that time, the world of literature was also available to a greater number of authors. This development was not unanimously accepted. As Count Dracula was falling, thus illustrating the end of the privilege of literature by and for a selected few, others saw these signs of democratization as signs of a bleak future for literature.

'The gentleman scholar' who still flourished when I was young, has sunken into unimportance both as reader and writer. The bagman and the stockbroker's clerk (and their lady wives and daughters) 'ave usurped his plyce and his influence as readers; and the pressman has picked up his fallen pen,—the pressman, sir, or the presswoman' (quoted by McDonald: 1)[6].

---

6   McDonald here quotes Henry Harland. 'Books: A Letter to the Editor and an Offer of a Prize', YB October 1895: 128.

Whatever Gosse thought of it, the world of letters was changing in Britain, giving space to many more people to write their own book, to write their own metaphors and re-describe the world as they saw it.

Bibliography

Stoker, Bram.' *Dracula. London*': Penguin Popular Classics. (1994).

Argoud, Line. *'Corps, conceptualisation, émergence du sens'*. Saint-Etienne: Publications de l'Université de Saint-Etienne, 2012.

Belford, Barbara. *'Bram Stoker, a Biography of the Author of Dracula'*. New York: Alfred A. Knopf (1996).

Hustis, Harriet. *'Black and White and Read All Over: Performative Textuality in Bram Stoker's Dracula'* in *'Studies in the Novel'*, Vol. 33, n°1 (Spring 2001), University of North Texas.

McDonald, Peter. *'British Literary Culture and Publishing Practice'* (1880-1914). Cambridge: Cambridge University Press (1997).

Ricoeur, Paul. *'La métaphore vive'*. Paris: Seuils (1975).

Seed, David. *'The Narrative Method of Dracula'* in *Nineteenth Century Fiction'*, Vol 40, N° 1 (June 1985), pp. 61-75, University of California Press.

Starr, Douglas. *'Blood, An Epic History of Medicine and Commerce'*. Little, Brown and Company, London, 1998.

Weedon, Alexis. *'Victorian Publishing, The Economics of Book Producion for a Mass Market'*, 1836-1916. Farnham: Ashgate (2003).

Wicke, Jennifer. *'Typewriting: Dracula and Its Media'* in ELH, Vol 59, N°2 (Summer, 1992), pp. 467-493. The John Hopkins University Press.

'A WONDERFUL MACHINE'

PHONOGRAPHY, TECHNOLOGY AND RECORDING IN BRAM STOKER'S DRACULA

R J E RILEY

'A WONDERFUL MACHINE'
PHONOGRAPHY, TECHNOLOGY AND RECORDING IN BRAM STOKER'S DRACULA

1 Transcribed Vampires

'How much tape did you bring?' asks Louis de Pointe du Lac at the start of Anne Rice's *'Interview with the Vampire'* (1976), *'enough for the story of a life?'*

For oral historian, Alessandro Portelli, this encounter exemplifies some of the epistemological, methodological and even ethical considerations that lie at the heart of his discipline. He reads the interview context as a potentially troubling instance of mutual vampirism. A speaker is voraciously recorded producing material that is potentially subject to a variety of archival appropriations. What also emerges is a persistent hauntological voice that can be found parasitically *'nesting within'* the historian's subsequent mediations.[1] When taken as a conceit that opens *'The Vampire Chronicles'* (1976-2003), however, Portelli laments that Rice fails to develop the implications of this *'wonderful idea'*. Once the interviewer disappears under du Lac's *'first person monologic narrative'* the novel loses the *'opportunity to connect the vampire's undead existence after death with the metaphoric implications of the recorded voice.'* [2]

That Rice does not accept her own thematic challenge could simply be attributed to reasons of narrative expediency. Her framing device is primarily pragmatic rather than overtly symbolic. Du Lac, and more precisely his memory, is the novel's main narrative force, and Rice works to immediately provide

---

1   Alessandro Portelli, 'Endpiece: We're All on Tape: Voice Recording and the Electronic Afterlife,' in *Between Generations: Family Models, Myths and Memories*, ed. by Daniel Bertaux and Paul Thompson (Oxford: Oxford University Press, 1993), 217.

2   Ibid.

him with an appropriate modus operandi: a contemporary context, an internal interlocutor and thus a reason for speaking. Thinking more speculatively, one could argue that the idea Portelli finds so fascinating, the concatenation of vampirism— recording and recording technology had already been subject to an extensive literary excavation prior to the publication of Rice's text. Indeed, in response to his criticism, she might have asked what more could be added to the theme in the light of its treatment in the most famous vampire novel of all, Bram Stoker's *'Dracula'* (1897)?

'Dracula', for all its melodrama, is a novel of technological contemporaneity. As a range of critics, including Friedrich Kittler, Jennifer Wicke and Leanne Page, have pointed out, it offers an epistolary narrative by way of Wilkie Collins that is grounded in the communicative materiality of the late nineteenth century. The letters and journal entries that constitute its transcribed sequence of 'papers' are pervaded with references to the operation of documentary, administrative and representational media such as typewriters, photographs, telegrams and phonographs.[3] The presence of the latter device represents, as Page reminds us, the primary evidence of the novel's intention to be *'up-to-date with a vengeance'* (39), having only been invented in the wax form used by Dr. Seward in 1888, two years before Stoker began preparing the text in 1890.[4]

When attempting to interpret this specialized content two trajectories are often posited, similar to the symbolic bipolarity outlined by Portelli. 'Technology' is read either as a register that stands in for, or exists in opposition to, the matrix of ideas signified by the word 'Dracula'.[5] In particular, the phonograph often occupies an alternating symbolic position, oscillating in critical discourse between the status of vampiric analogue and signifier of scientific rationality. It is seen to consume the voice while also offering an

---

3   Bram Stoker, *'Dracula'* ed. by Roger Luckhurst (Oxford: Oxford University Press, 2011), 5. Future quotations will come from this volume and will be identified in the text using D.

4   Leanne Page, *'Phonograph, Shorthand, Typewriter: High Performance Technologies in Bram Stoker's Dracula'*, *Victorian Network* 3.2 (2011): 98.

5   For an account of this ambivalence, see Luckhurst's introduction to his 2011 edition of *'Dracula'* (vii-xxxii) xxix-xxxi.

empirical functionality antithetical to the folkloric status of a supernatural figure.[6]

The contention in each case is that Stoker's representational logic is built on a structure of metaphoric polarisation. In part, this mode of reading works as a critical strategy of positive evaluation because 'Dracula' is often seen to hold an ambivalent position as a literary 'classic'. In response to claims concerning its purple prose and shallow characterization, the novel's formal construction is often privileged. As Christopher Frayling argues, 'Dracula' is not *just a pile of pieces of information about the author* but *a structure held together well below the surface of the text*.[7] The claim that its technological register carries symbolic resonance reiterates this assessment. It aligns the composition of its narrative architecture with linguistic and, by extension, artistic 'depth'.

Having said this, there is something curious about this aspect of 'Dracula' and its critical reception. Despite the novel's ability to sustain a wealth of theoretically informed socio-political readings, its metaphorical economy exhibits no more development over the course of its narrative than that of 'Interview with a Vampire'. Stoker creates a narrow semiosis due to the novel's expositionary mode of articulation. The significance and complexity of 'Dracula' is right there on the surface. There is very little in the way of subtext. Dracula is a 'foreigner', he is a capitalist and he is a figure of the supernatural. This is a novel about blood, sexuality and infection because these are the substances, impulses and processes that the protagonists explicitly experience, discuss and wrestle. Similarly, the themes of property law, psychiatry and natural philosophy are linked to a set of clearly delineated character professions and become apparent in the text due to the execution of these roles across the ostensible plot.

This specificity applies equally to Stoker's representation of technology and particularly that of the phonograph. The device is an integral aspect of his conceit of the transcribed document. It acts as an operative part of the novel's foregrounded textual

---

6   This is the oscillation performed by Wicke, Page and Terry Scarborough, discussed below. Similar ideas can also be found in Judith Halberstam, 'Skin Shows: Gothic Horror and the Technology of Monsters' (Durham: Duke University Press, 1995).

7   Christopher Frayling,' Vampyres: Lord Byron to Count Dracula' (London: Faber, 1991), 302. Emphasis in original.

production and its significance can be connected to its material functionality rather than its symbolic value. The signifying logic of *'Dracula'* is not primarily metaphorical but metonymic. Meaning is generated not through implied symbolic extension but through the accumulation of concepts via association. When considering the connection Stoker establishes between the *'vampire's undead existence'* and *'the metaphoric implications of the recorded voice'*, we should re-calibrate the rhetorical trope applied as a framework of interpretation. One should analyse what the represented object does in the text just as much as what it symbolises in excess of the novel's ostensible content.

2 Metaphor And Metonymy

The distinction between metaphor and metonymy in respect to the construction of literary discourse is a formalist principle originally defined by Roman Jakobson. Metaphor and metonymy are both rhetorical tropes that describe one thing via reference to another. They can also be seen as distinct signifying processes that generate meaning differently within the space of the sentence. Metaphor involves the substitution of terms across registers on the basis of a perceived similarity. For Jakobson, the production and recognition of metaphor involves the negotiation of the vertical axis of language. One term or phrase within a sentence is exchanged for another from a parallel semantic field. Metaphorical signification is thus a strategy of importation that involves the intersection of a sentence with ostensibly incongruous discourses. In contrast, metonymy is described as horizontal in its operation because it connects ideas and topics via contiguity. The description of a whole through reference to an attribute or, in the case of synecdoche, a part, requires associative reference rather than substitution. It is a figurative mode centred upon conceptual proximity.[8]

---

8   See Roman Jakobson, 'Two Aspects of Language and Two Types of Aphasic Disturbances,' in 'Fundamentals of Language '(The Hague: Mouton, 1971), 66; 'The development of a discourse may take place along two different semantic lines: one topic may lead to another either through their similarity or through their contiguity. The metaphoric way would be the most appropriate term for the first case and the metonymic way for the second, since they find their most condensed expression in metaphor and metonymy respectively.'

For example, when Jonathan Harker states that Dracula lay *'like a filthy leech, exhausted with his repletion'* (51), 'leech' functions as a metaphor. The claim is not that Dracula has transformed but that he exhibits an engorgement similar to that of the post-feeding state of another blood dependent creature. The image carries further allusions of parasitism and disgust but this negative tenor remains comparative as the metaphorical vehicle operates in relation to the paralleling fulcrum of 'like'. In contrast, Dr. Seward's later descriptions of the Count's *'hellish look'*, his eyes of *'devilish passion'* (262) and *'the diabolical quickness of* [his] *leap'* (284) are acts of metonymic labelling. The terms describe actions and attributes through the use of a consistent adjectival register. This 'satanic' language can easily be associated with the general register of the supernatural signified by 'vampire'. More specifically, when 'Dracula' is read as a proper noun taken from a pre-existant concrete noun, the Wallacian word for 'Devil', the adjectives appear contiguous with their point of reference, not the result of vertical substitution.[9] They operate as markers of Seward's rhetorical intensification complete with a distinct tenor of evil and immorality but this is achieved not through comparison with that which Dracula is *like* but via a reiteration of that which, in the world of the novel, he actually *is*.

For Jakobson, the generation of literary discourse involves the creative negotiation of these two axes, a movement that is due to the connotative capacity of language. Critics such as David Lodge have used this understanding to define literary realism as a metonymic discourse while critiquing parallel interpretations of the form on the basis of their metaphorical projections.[10] A similar point could be made as regards readings of *'Dracula'*. Robert Eighteen-Bisang and Elizabeth Miller see the novel as a *'study in opposition'* in which Stoker constructs a series of thematic binaries including *'science vs. supernatural'* and

---

9   According to Frayling, Stoker read William Wilkinson's *'Account of the Principalities of Wallachia and Moldavia'* (1820) during his research in which he found the name *'Dracula'* and its etymology. (319).

10   David Lodge, *'Analysis and Interpretation of the Realist Text: A Pluralistic Approach to Ernest Hemingway's 'Cat in the Rain' Poetics Today* 1.4 (1980): 10.

'*technology vs. magic*'.[11] In support of this overview, they cite Ronald Morrison's description of the 'tension' Stoker establishes between the '*gothic supernatural elements and the scientific advances of the late Victorian age*'.[12]

For Terry Scarborough, this is a tension that is resolved in the circumventing dominance of the supernatural polarity over that of the scientific. He sees the text as one in which '*atavistic superstition resurfaces in a problematizing assault*' on Victorian assumptions of '*technological omnipotence*'.[13] This contention is communicated directly through the epistolary structure that is wedded so distinctly to '*the type-writer, the phonograph, the telegraph and the Kodak*.'[14] Dracula inhabits the lacunae that the novel's obsessive documentation leaves open, '*the very spaces that enlightenment cannot illuminate*.'[15]

Certainly this is implied through Dracula's attack on Mina in Chapter 21. The Count descends and forces her to drink his blood while Harker, Seward and Van Helsing are elsewhere, interrogating Renfield. The assault functions as a libidinal act of vampiric consumption/copulation as well as a tactical strike upon the recording capacity of the group. Dracula burns the archive of manuscripts and phonograph cylinders before rendering Mina, the fastidious secretary, '*mad with terror*' (263) after making her, in her own words, 'unclean' (264). Such sabotage dramatises what Scarborough identifies as the novel's representation of epistemological destabilization. For all the empirical precision highlighted in the use of documentary media to survey, map, record and transcribe information relevant to Dracula's movements, these processes ultimately seem vulnerable to the occult practices of their subject. The Count's ability to invade and subvert before disappearing in a '*faint vapour*' (262) signifies what Scarborough would term the '*fissures in scientific*

---

11   Eighteen-Bisang, Robert and Elizabeth, '*Bram Stoker's Notes for Dracula: A Facsimile Edition*' (London: McFarland, 2008), 292.

12   Ibid.

13   Terry Scarborough, '*Science or Séance?: Late-Victorian Science and Dracula's Epistolary Structure*' (2008), http://www.victorianweb.org/authors/stoker/scarborough1.html (accessed October 15th 2012), para. 11 of 12.

14   Ibid., para. 2 of 12.

15   Ibid., para. 8 of 12.

and technological progress through which speculation threatens scientific authority'.[16]

This argument is similar to that proposed by Page. She sees *'Dracula'* as a text in which *'communication technologies fail to perform as asked by their users'.* Page's discussion relates to *'techno-performance'* as it is understood in terms of signifying functionality.[17] Her concern is with Stoker's depiction of contemporaneous recording media in operation, the manner in which, for example, *'characters are often forced to shift from using one technology to another'* for reasons of practical efficacy, a movement that augments their *'performances of research and journal writing'.*[18] This post-Kittler materialist reading can be used to foreground the problematics involved in Scarborough's thematic discussion of technological failure. Page locates the technology of *'Dracula'* as a described prosthesis rather than a represented analogue. The emphasis is placed on the significance of operational praxis in the narrative. In contrast, Scarborough's trajectory extrapolates a symbolic extension from the generalized signifier 'technology' so as to posit a wider metaphorical schema of *'darkness against enlightenment'.*[19] Characters, objects and procedures are taken as signifiers that stand-in for abstract concepts of knowledge reflective of a late-Victorian epistemological paradigm. The problem with this model is that its totalising extension erases the operational specificity of the represented technology that constitutes the metaphor's vehicle. Typewriters, cameras and phonographs all became ciphers of 'science' and 'progress'. In addition, the development of this register into a binary opposition with parallel concepts drawn from 'vampire' and *'Dracula'* construct an antithetical model that is not borne out by the novel's content.

---

16   Ibid., para. 2 of 12.

17   Page, 96.

18   Page, 105.

19   Scarborough, para. 4 of 12.

3 Technological Transcription And Supernatural Identity

In his original composition notes, compiled between 1890 and 1896, Stoker does initially point to a narrative structure and thematic organization centred upon diametric opposition. He did initially hypothesize an unrepresentable Dracula. When listing possible characteristics Stoker states that the Count *'could not Codak'* [sic] and that any photograph would *'come out black or like a skeleton corpse'.*[20] In what is widely regarded as a nod to Oscar Wilde's, *'The Picture of Dorian Gray'* (1891), Stoker also suggested that Dracula could not be depicted in paint, any portrait made would appear as *'someone else'.*[21] In parallel to the development of this profile, Stoker was also outlining his supporting cast, which initially included one Alfred Singleton, a *'Psychical Research Agent'.*[22] The specificity of this profession is indicative of an allusion to the then recently formed Society for Psychical Research. Founded in London in 1882, the SPR was concerned with the study of parapsychological phenomena. Emerging in parallel with and partly in response to the wider cultural interest in Theosophy and Spiritualism, the society was scientific in its methodology and frequently critical in its results.[23] Its researchers would often make use of photography and phonography during their investigations to validate individuals and processes apparently able to yield such 'evidence' as spirit photographs.[24] By casting a character indicative of this parapsychological milleu alongside an entity recalcitrant to representational mediation, Stoker seems to have initially based his project, *'The Un-Dead'*, around a counterpoint between an empirical gaze of documentation and Dracula's ability to circumvent such attempts at generating material evidence.

This embryonic scenario anticipates William Hope Hodgson's

---

20 Eighteen-Bisang and Miller, 21.

21 Ibid., 25.

22 Ibid., 27.

23 See Renee Haynes, *'The Society Physical Research: A History, 1882-1982'* (London: Macdonald, 1982).

24 For example, Arthur Palliser suggests that the phonograph could prove a useful tool of investigation in *'Do Animals See Ghosts?'* *Journal of the Society for Psychical Research* IV.LXL (1889): 95. An unsigned note in the March 1888 issue of the *Journal* (III.XLVIIL), *'Experiments in Hypnotism'* discusses the experimental efficacy of photographic equipment. (235).

stories of the *'psychic detective'*, Thomas Carnacki. In *'The Whistling Room'* (1909), Carnacki pursues a recording methodology and achieves results similar to those we might have expected of Singleton:

'I tried to get a phonographic record of the whistling; but it simply produced no impression on the wax at all. That is one of the things that has made me feel queer, I can tell you. Another extraordinary thing is that the microphone will not magnify the sound—will not even transmit it; it seems to take no account of it, and acts if it were nonexistent'.[25]

What appears in the completed version of *'Dracula'*, however, is the exact opposite of this counterpoint structure. Singleton, the Psychical Research Agent, is absorbed into Van Helsing, the natural philosopher, who possesses very little technical skill. In contrast to Carnacki, Dr. Seward's phonograph is a supplementary device rather than an investigative tool. It occupies the position of a 'notebook', providing an efficient personal space where he can *'keep [his] diary'* (205).[26] What we see in the story of Hodgson is a technological failure due to the inability of a device to function in the face of supernatural phenomena. Seward pursues no comparable strategy of instrumentalization. It is *'entirely—almost entirely about [his] cases'* (205). The phonograph is used to record Seward's own narration of his encounters with Dracula and Renfield. It is not used to record either of them as documentary subjects. As a result, it occupies a non-confrontational and thus non-antithetical position in relation to the former. Dracula's spectral insubstantial presence in the otherwise polyphonic text occurs not because he is ontologically resistant to representation (he writes, his speech is often transcribed). The novel's photographic and phonographic apertures, though, are never directed towards him. Unlike the Dracula of Fred Saberhagen's, *'The Dracula Tape'* (1975), the Count is never seen to utilise audio/visual recording technology nor is he subject to such recordings.

---

25 William Hope Hodgson, 'The Whistling Room' [1909], in Carnacki: 'The Ghost Finder' (Great Britain: Wordsworth, 2009), 82.

26 Bisang and Miller report that in his notes, Stoker first refers to Seward's documentary as a 'diary notebook', 101.

The only residue of Stoker's original character design is Dracula's lack of reflection. This quality, by all accounts Stoker's own addition to the vampire myth, is first noted by Harker in Chapter 2. As Jennifer Wicke comments, it is easy to read this status as indicative of a wider unrecordable nature:

[...] if a vampire's image cannot be captured in a mirror, photographs of a vampire might prove equally disappointing. That scary absence from the sphere of the photographable shunts the anxiety back onto vampirism itself: vampirism as a stand-in for the uncanny procedures of modern life.[27]

Here, Wicke reads a denoted character detail as a connotative symbol before going on to see in Stoker the operation of a third-order signification. The presumed implication of the mirror, its apparent substitution in place of the photograph, is taken as an index of the metaphorical logic carried by vampirism. Vampirism equates to uncanny modernity because Dracula resists photography and this is only known because he cannot be seen in a mirror.

This is an astute argument but the chain of connotation upon which it rests is problematised by two connected factors— Stoker's point of reference that informs his inclusion of the mirror and the manner in which this specificity contrasts with the operation of the other apparatus of the novel. To take the first point, Stoker's research notes contain quotations from George Cheyne's *'The English Malady'* (1733). This medical treatise describes, amongst other anomalies and diseases, the *'nephritic complaint'* a state of *'dying and coming to life at pleasure'*. Stoker cites Cheyne's observations of the phenomenon that includes the expected symptoms: *'No motion of the heart. Mirror held over mouth not even soiled etc.'*[28] The use of a mirror to check for signs of breath is a standard procedure of medical verification. In *'Dracula'*, Stoker appears to have amplified this

---

27   Jennifer Wicke, 'Vampiric Typewriting: 'Dracula' and Its Media' ELH 59.2 (1992): 473.

28   Eighteen-Bisang and Miller, 239.

lack of an organic trace in line with the ambiguity of the Count's undead status. Dracula inhabits an extreme and paradoxical state in which he is neither alive nor dead. He is neither fully human nor is he a re-animated corpse. He occupies an alien ontology, a post-mortem state in which he has undergone death but remains a tangible animate thinking entity. The character is presented in the absence of a visible trace because, as nosferatu, he is nothing but a trace, a *'man-that- was'* (224). Van Helsing resists using the present tense third person *'he is'*. Dracula's lack of reflection visually signifies a similar first person circumvention of identity categorization. His negative encounter with the mirror points to an identity that lies beyond the boundaries of definition signalled by the self-consciousness and self-perception of *'I am'*.

It does not automatically follow that the novel's overt indications of a supernatural status metaphorically equate to a wider characterization of representational recalcitrance. The mirror is not a signifying device of the same order as the phonograph or photograph. It reflects an image in the presence of a subject rather than creating an imitation via an analogical process of transformation. This difference is important when attempting to understand Stoker's vampiric taxonomy and its role in the narrative of *'Dracula'*. Although the Count does not reflect, he nevertheless functions through a process of reproduction. As is suggested by *'Vampires in New England'*, an 1896 *'New York World'* article contained in Stoker's research notes, the vampire is a figure of plague. It survives through parasitic activity that is replicated in the victim who becomes 'night prowler in pursuit of human prey'.[29] Similarly, Lucy Westenra is not killed by Dracula but vampirized, causing her to imitate his behaviour and also to embody a comparable trace structure. In Chapter 16, when Lucy is discovered in the tomb prior to her destruction, Holmwood asks if he is seeing *'Lucy's body'* or *'a demon in her shape'*. In an anticipation of his description of Dracula, Van Helsing replies that he will see her as *'she was and is'* because it is *'her body and yet not it'* (199).

---

29 Ibid.,191.

Vampirism as replication: such imitation finds direct parallel in Stoker's description of phonographic recording. In Chapter 17, Mina begins to transcribe Seward's wax cylinders, doing what Freud could not or would not do. She analyses the recorded narrative of a speaker finding latent content beyond that which Seward 'intended' (207).[30] His recorded voice, which Mina initially mistakes for another speaker, thus repeats the uncanny dissonance of the vampiric state. The reproduced content of the wax cylinder is Dr. Seward and is not Dr. Seward at the same time. The device yields a voice that carries in its tone and replayable intonation an unruly significance that is neutralised by the silence of the typewritten script. Wicke reads this foregrounded transition not in terms of an opposition between speech and writing but as evidence of Stoker's presentation of speech *already colonized or vampirized by mass mediation*.[31] This use of vampirism as a metaphor to connote mass mediation obscures the isomorphism that Stoker established between the instances of replication. Dracula's self-perpetuation and Seward's phonograph recordings are activities that mirror each other. Both involve the production of copies, and both are negated through the dissolution of the heart, a stake through the heart in the case of Lucy and an erasure of the audible *'heart beat'* (207) in the case of Seward's phonograph disclosure. In contrast to the substitution that Wicke identifies in this equivalence, the connectivity between the procedures is metonymic.

The parallelism is established on the basis of a contiguous association. The recordings that Mina transcribes contain Seward's personal thoughts about Lucy, her vampirism and destruction, a narrative that traumatically resonates with Mina upon hearing it. This instance of recording, transcription and transference is then not just imagistically equivalent to Dracula's activity in the novel but directly prompted by it. There is a structure of cause and effect

---

30   Freud invests the phonograph and the gramophone with a certain imaginative economy at various points during his work. In his 'Dora' case study ('*Fragments of an Analysis of a Case of Hysteria*' (1905) [1901]), however, Freud valorises his own memorial processes of post-session transcription rather than the potential use of the phonograph during the psychoanalytic session. See Sigmund Freud, '*Case Histories: Dora and Little Hans*' ed. by Angela Richards *et al* (Harmondsworth: Penguin, 1977). Kittler analyses the overlaps between '*Dracula*', technology and psychoanalysis in '*Gramophone, Film, Typewriter*', 87-92.

31   Wicke, 471.

within the narrative that horizontally links Stoker's depiction of reproductive processes. While each activity, the material and the supernatural, the informational and the vampiric, can separately be interpreted as an index of a wider metaphorical register, Stoker's plotting and Wilkie Collins's narrative style brings each into proximity through non-polarised association. This reading can be taken further in the light of Page's observation that the typewriter occupies the role of a 'metatechnology' in *'Dracula'*.[32] Because the text is offered to the reader as a dossier of typescripts, the typewriter with its manifold duplication function constitutes the primary media through which the novel's multiplatform data is filtered. This mediation includes engagement with two forms of phonography over the course of the novel, Seward's wax cylinders and Harker's journal, *'kept in shorthand'* (5). What then appears to constitute the 'structure' that Frayling privileges is a successive sequence of mediations. Stoker does not just refer to plural technologies during the course of the novel but instead constructs a bureaucratic narrative in which one system of imitation feeds into and is processed by another. This is a chain, I would argue, that includes the process of vampirism.

'Dracula' is a novel that is complex enough to support polyvalent readings. This complexity, however, is a product of its detailed focus on seemingly opposed conceptual spheres, the supernatural and the technological. What connects these representations is a consistent emphasis on the action of reproduction. As the novel progresses, the reader is taken through an associative sequence of written text, audio reproduction and self-replication within a wider foregrounded framework of re-formatted typescript. Stoker's artistic depth rests upon this architecture. Whilst its literary verticality continues to expand in critical discourse it is this horizontal concern with the ontology of the copy that forms the foundation of the novel.

---

32   Page, 109.

Bibliography

Primary

Hope Hodgson, William, Carnacki: ' The Ghost Finder' [1909] (Hertfordshire: Wordsworth, 2009).

Rice, Ann, 'Interview with a Vampire' (New York: Knopf, 1976).

Saberhagen, Fred, 'The Dracula Tape' (New York: Warner,1975).

Stoker, Bram,' Dracula' ed. by Roger Luckhurst [1897] (Oxford: Oxford University Press, 2011).

Secondary

Bertaux, Daniel and Paul Thompson (eds.), 'Between Generations: Family Models, Myths and Memories' (Oxford: Oxford University Press, 1993).

Eighteen-Bisang, Robert and Elizabeth Miller, 'Bram Stoker's Notes for 'Dracula': A Facsimile Edition' (London: McFarland, 2008).

Frayling, Christopher, 'Vampyres: Lord Byron to Count Dracula' (London: Faber, 1991).

Freud, Sigmund, 'Case Histories: Dora and Little Hans' ed. by Angela Richards et al (Harmondsworth: Penguin, 1977).

Halberstam, Judith, 'Skin Shows: Gothic Horror and the Technology of Monsters' (Durham: Duke University Press, 1995).

Haining, Peter, 'The Dracula Centenary Book' (London: Souvenir Press, 1987).

Haynes, Renee, 'The Society Physical Research: A History, 1882-1982' (London: Macdonald, 1982).

Jakobson, Roman, 'Two Aspects of Language and Two Types of Aphasic Disturbances,' in 'Fundamentals of Language' (The Hague: Mouton, 1971).

Kittler, Friedrich, 'Gramophone, Film, Typewriter' trans. Geoffrey Winthrop-Young and Michael Wutz (Stanford: Stanford University Press, 1999).

Lodge, David, 'Analysis and Interpretation of the Realist Text: A Pluralistic Approach to Ernest Hemingway's 'Cat in the Rain'' Poetics Today 1.4 (1980), 5-22.

Page, Leanne, 'Phonograph, Shorthand, Typewriter: High Performance Technologies in Bram Stoker's Dracula', Victorian Network 3.2 (2011), 95-113.

Scarborough, Terry, 'Science or Séance?: Late-Victorian Science and Dracula's Epistolary Structure' (2008), http://www.victorianweb.org/authors/stoker/scarborough1.html

Wicke, Jennifer, 'Vampiric Typewriting: Dracula and Its Media' ELH 59.2 (1992), 467-493.

EXTRACTS FROM 'DRACULA'

BRAM STOKER

EXTRACTS FROM 'DRACULA'
BY BRAM STOKER

JONATHAN HARKER'S JOURNAL

Later: the morning of 16 May.— I suppose I must have fallen asleep; I hope so, but I fear, for all that followed was startlingly real—so real that now, sitting here in the broad, full sunlight of the morning, I cannot in the least believe that it was all sleep.

I was not alone. The room was the same, unchanged in any way since I came into it; I could see along the floor, in the brilliant moonlight, my own footsteps marked where I had disturbed the long accumulation of dust. In the moonlight opposite me were three young women, ladies by their dress and manner. I thought at the time that I must be dreaming when I saw them, for, though the moonlight was behind them, they threw no shadow on the floor. They came close to me and looked at me for some time and then whispered together. Two were dark, and had high aquiline noses, like the Count's, and great dark, piercing eyes, that seemed to be almost red when contrasted with the pale yellow moon. The other was fair, as fair as can be, with great, wavy masses of golden hair and eyes like pale sapphires. I seemed somehow to know her face, and to know it in connection with some dreamy fear, but I could not recollect at the moment how or where. All three had brilliant white teeth, that shone like pearls against the ruby of their voluptuous lips. There was something about them that made me uneasy, some longing and at the same time some deadly fear. I felt in my heart a wicked, burning desire that they would kiss me with those red lips. It is not good to note this down, lest some day it should meet Mina's eyes and cause her pain; but it is the truth. They whispered together, and then they all three laughed—such a silvery, musical laugh, but as hard as though the sound never could have come through the softness of human lips. It was like the intolerable, tingling sweetness of water-glasses when played on by a cunning hand. The fair girl shook her head coquettishly, and the other two urged her on. One said:—

'Go on! You are first, and we shall follow; yours is the right to begin.' The other added:—

'He is young and strong; there are kisses for us all.' I lay quiet, looking out under my eyelashes in an agony of delightful anticipation. The fair girl advanced and bent over me till I could feel the movement of her breath upon me. Sweet it was in one sense, honey-sweet, and sent the same tingling through the nerves as her voice, but with a bitter underlying the sweet, a bitter offensiveness, as one smells in blood.

I was afraid to raise my eyelids, but looked out and saw perfectly under the lashes. The fair girl went on her knees and bent over me, fairly gloating. There was a deliberate voluptuousness which was both thrilling and repulsive, and as she arched her neck she actually licked her lips like an animal, till I could see in the moonlight the moisture shining on the scarlet lips and on the red tongue as it lapped the white sharp teeth. Lower and lower went her head as the lips went below the range of my mouth and chin and seemed about to fasten on my throat. Then she paused, and I could hear the churning sound of her tongue as it licked her teeth and lips, and could feel the hot breath on my neck. Then the skin of my throat began to tingle as one's flesh does when the hand that is to tickle it approaches nearer—nearer. I could feel the soft, shivering touch of the lips on the supersensitive skin of my throat, and the hard dents of two sharp teeth, just touching and pausing there. I closed my eyes in a languorous ecstasy and waited—waited with beating heart.

DR SEWARD'S DIARY
(Kept in phonograph)

25 April.—Ebb tide in appetite to-day. Cannot eat, cannot rest, so diary instead. Since my rebuff of yesterday I have a sort of empty feeling; nothing in the world seems of sufficient importance to be worth the doing. . . . As I knew that the only cure for this sort of thing was work, I went down amongst the patients. I picked out one who has afforded me a study of much interest. He is so quaint in his ideas, and so unlike the normal lunatic, that I have determined to understand him as well as I can. To-day I seemed to get nearer than ever before to the heart of his mystery.

I questioned him more fully than I had ever done, with a view to making myself master of the facts of his hallucination. In my manner of doing it there was, I now see, something of cruelty. I seemed to wish to keep him to the point of his madness—a thing which I avoid with the patients as I would the mouth of hell. (*Mem.*, under what circumstances would I *not* avoid the pit of hell?) *Omnia Romae venalia sunt.* Hell has its price! *verb. sap.* If there be anything behind this instinct it will be valuable to trace it afterwards *accurately*, so I had better commence to do so, therefore—

R. M. Renfield, aetat. 59—Sanguine temperament; great physical strength; morbidly excitable; periods of gloom ending in some fixed idea which I cannot make out. I presume that the sanguine temperament itself and the disturbing influence end in a mentally-accomplished finish; a possibly dangerous man, probably dangerous if unselfish. In selfish men caution is as secure an armour for their foes as for themselves. What I think of on this point is, when self is the fixed point the centripetal force is balanced with the centrifugal: when duty, a cause, etc., is the fixed point, the latter force is paramount, and only accident or a series of accidents can balance it.

Whitby.

MINA MURRAY'S JOURNAL

9 August.—The sequel to the strange arrival of the derelict in the storm last night is almost more startling than the thing itself. It turns out that the schooner is a Russian from Varna, and is called the *Demeter*. She is almost entirely in ballast of silver sand, with only a small amount of cargo—a number of great wooden boxes filled with mould. This cargo was consigned to a Whitby solicitor, Mr S. F. Billington, of 7, The Crescent, who this morning went aboard and formally took possession of the goods consigned to him. The Russian consul, too, acting for the charter-party, took formal possession of the ship, and paid all harbour dues, etc. Nothing is talked about here to-day except the strange coincidence; the officials of the Board of Trade have been most exacting in seeing that every compliance has been made with existing regulations. As the matter is to be a 'nine days' wonder,' they are evidently determined that there shall be no cause of after complaint. A good deal of interest was abroad concerning the dog which landed when the ship struck, and more than a few of the members of the S.P.C.A., which is very strong in Whitby, have tried to befriend the animal. To the general disappointment, however, it was not to be found; it seems to have disappeared entirely from the town. It may be that it was frightened and made its way on to the moors, where it is still hiding in terror. There are some who look with dread on such a possibility, lest later on it should in itself become a danger, for it is evidently a fierce brute. Early this morning a large dog, a half-bred mastiff, belonging to a coal merchant close to Tate Hill Pier, was found dead in the roadway opposite its master's yard. It had been fighting, and manifestly had had a savage opponent, for its throat was torn away, and its belly slit open as if with a savage claw.

Letter, Samuel F. Billington & Son, Solicitors, Whitby,
to Messrs. Carter, Paterson & Co., London

'*17 August.*

'Dear Sirs,—

'Herewith please receive invoice of goods sent by Great Northern Railway. Same are to be delivered to Carfax, near Purfleet, immediately on receipt at goods station King's Cross. The house is at present empty, but enclosed please find keys, all of which are labelled.

'You will please deposit the boxes, fifty in number, which form the consignment, in the partially ruined building forming part of the house and marked "A" on rough diagram enclosed. Your agent will easily recognize the locality, as it is the ancient chapel of the mansion. The goods leave by the train at 9.30 to-night, and will be due at King's Cross at 4.30 to-morrow afternoon. As our client wishes the delivery made as soon as possible, we shall be obliged by your having teams ready at King's Cross at the time named and forthwith conveying the goods to destination. In order to obviate any delays possible through any routine requirements as to payment in your departments, we enclose cheque herewith for ten pounds (£10), receipt of which please acknowledge. Should the charge be less than this amount, you can return balance; if greater, we shall at once send cheque for difference on hearing from you. You are to leave the keys on coming away in the main hall of the house, where the proprietor may get them on his entering the house by means of his duplicate key.

'Pray do not take us as exceeding the bounds of business courtesy in pressing you in all ways to use the utmost expedition.

'We are, dear Sirs,

'Faithfully yours,

'SAMUEL F. BILLINGTON & SON'.

LUCY WESTENRA'S DIARY

Hillingham, 24 August—I must imitate Mina, and keep writing things down. Then we can have long talks when we do meet. I wonder when it will be. I wish she were with me again, for I feel so unhappy. Last night I seemed to be dreaming again just as I was at Whitby. Perhaps it is the change of air, or getting home again. It is all dark and horrid to me, for I can remember nothing; but I am full of vague fear, and I feel so weak and worn out. When Arthur came to lunch he looked quite grieved when he saw me, and I hadn't the spirit to be cheerful. I wonder if I could sleep in mother's room to-night. I shall make an excuse and try.

25 August.— Another bad night. Mother did not seem to take to my proposal. She seems not too well herself, and doubtless she fears to worry me. I tried to keep awake, and succeeded for a while; but when the clock struck twelve it waked me from a doze, so I must have been falling asleep. There was a sort of scratching or flapping at the window, but I did not mind it, and as I remember no more, I suppose I must then have fallen asleep. More bad dreams. I wish I could remember them. This morning I am horribly weak. My face is ghastly pale, and my throat pains me. It must be something wrong with my lungs, for I don't seem ever to get air enough. I shall try to cheer up when Arthur comes, or else I know he will be miserable to see me so.

'The Pall Mall Gazette,' 18 September

THE ESCAPED WOLF
PERILOUS ADVENTURE OF OUR INTERVIEWER
Interview with the Keeper in the Zoological Gardens

After many inquiries and almost as many refusals, and perpetually using the words *Pall Mall Gazette* as a sort of talisman I managed to find the keeper of the section of the Zoological Gardens in which the wolf department is included. Thomas Bilder lives in one of the cottages in the enclosure behind the elephant-house, and was just sitting down to his tea when I found him. Thomas and his wife are hospitable folk, elderly, and without children, and if the specimen I enjoyed of their hospitality be of the average kind, their lives must be pretty comfortable.

The keeper would not enter on what he called 'business' until the supper was over, and we were all satisfied. Then when the table was cleared, and he had lit his pipe, he said:—

'Now, sir, you can go and arsk me what you want. You'll excoose me refoosin' to talk of perfeshunal subjects afore meals. I gives the wolves and the jackals and the hyenas in all our section their tea afore I begins to arsk them questions.'

'How do you mean, ask them questions?' I queried, wishing to get him into a talkative murmour.

''Ittin' of them over the 'ead with a pole is one way; scratchin' of their hears is another, when gents as is flush wants a bit of a show-orf to their gals. I don't so much mind the fust—the 'ittin' with a pole afore I chucks in their dinner; but I waits till they've 'ad their sherry and kawffee, so to speak, afore I tries on with the ear-scratchin'. Mind you,' he added philosophically , 'there's a deal of the same nature in us as in them there animiles. Here's you a-comin' and arskin' of me questions about my business, and I that grumpy-like that only for your bloomin' 'arf-quid I'd 'a' seen you blowed fust 'fore I'd answer. Not even when you arsked me sarcastic-like if I'd like you to arsk the Superintendent if you might arsk me questions. Without offence, did I tell yer to go to 'ell?'

'You did.'

'An' when you said you'd report me for usin' of obscene language, that was 'itten' me over the 'ead; but the 'arf-quid made that all right. I weren't a-goin' to fight, so I waited for the food, and did with my 'owl as the wolves, and lions, and tigers does. But, Lor' love yer 'art, now that the old 'ooman has stuck a chunk of her tea-cake in me, an' rinsed me out with her bloomin' old teapot, and I've lit up, you may scratch my ears for all you're worth, and won't get even a growl out of me. Drive along with your questions. I know what yer a-comin' at, that 'ere escaped wolf.'

'Exactly. I want you to give me your view of it. Just tell me how it happened; and when I know the facts I'll get you to say what you consider was the cause of it, and how you think the whole affair will end.'

'All right, guv'nor. This 'ere is about the 'ole story. That 'ere wolf what we called Bersicker was one of three grey ones that came from Norway to Jamrach's, which we bought off him four year ago. He was a nice well-behaved wolf, that never gave no trouble to talk of. I'm more surprised at 'im for wantin' to get out nor any other animile in the place. But, there, you can't trust wolves no more nor women.'

'Don't you mind him, sir!' broke in Mrs Tom, with a cheery laugh. "E's got mindin' the animiles so long that blest if he ain't like a old wolf 'isself! But there ain't no 'arm in 'im.'

'Well, sir, it was about two hours after feedin' yesterday when I first hear any disturbance. I was makin' up a litter in the monkey-house for a young puma which is ill; but when I heard the yelpin' and 'owlin' I kem away straight. There was Bersicker a-tearin' like a mad thing at the bars as if he wanted to get out. There wasn't much people about that day, and close at hand was only one man, a tall, thin chap, with a 'ook nose and a pointed beard, with a few white hairs runnin' through it. He had a 'ard, cold look and red eyes, and I took a sort of mislike to him, for it seemed as if it was 'im as they was hirritated at. He 'ad white kid gloves on 'is 'ands, and he pointed out the animiles to me and says: "Keeper, these wolves seem upset at something."

' "Maybe it's you," says I, for I did not like the airs as he give 'isself. He didn't get angry, as I 'oped he would but he smiled a kind of insolent smile, with a mouth full of white, sharp teeth. "Oh no, they wouldn't like me," 'e says.

' "Ow yes, they would,"says I, a-imitatin' of him. "They always like a bone or two to clean their teeth on about tea-time, which you 'as a bagful."

'Well, it was a odd thing, but when the animiles see us a-talkin' they lay down, and when I went over to Bersicker he let me stroke his ears same as ever. That there man kem over, and blessed but if he didn't put in his hand and stroke the old wolf's ears too!

' "Tyke care," says I. "Bersicker is quick."

' "Never mind,' he says. 'I'm used to 'em!"

' "Are you in the business yourself?" I says, tyking off my 'at, for a man what trades in wolves, anceterer, is a good friend to keepers.

' "No," says he, 'not exactly in the business, but I 'ave made pets of several." And with that he lifts his 'at as perlite as a lord, and walks away. Old Bersicker kep' a-lookin' arter 'im till 'e was out of sight, and then went and lay down in a corner, and wouldn't come hout the 'ole hevening. Well, larst night, so soon as the moon was hup, the wolves here all began a-'owling. There warn't nothing for them to 'owl at. There warn't no one near, except someone that was evidently a-callin' a dog somewheres out back of the gardings in the Park road. Once or twice I went out to see that all was right, and it was, and then the 'owling stopped. Just before twelve o'clock I just took a look round afore turnin' in, an', bust me, but when I kem opposite to old Bersicker's cage I see the rails broken and twisted about and the cage empty. And that's all I know for certing.'

'Did anyone else see anything?'

'One of our gard'ners was a-comin 'ome about that time from a 'armony, when he sees a big grey dog comin' out through the gardin 'edges. At least, so he says; but I don't give much for it myself, for if he did 'e never said a word about it to his missis when 'e got 'ome, and it was only after the escape of the wolf was made known, and we had been up all night a-huntin' of the Park for Bersicker, that he remembered seein' anything. My own belief was that the 'armony 'ad got into his 'ead.'

'Now, Mr Bilder, can you account in any way for the escape of the wolf?'

'Well, sir, he said, with a suspicious sort of modesty, 'I think I can; but I don't know as 'ow you'd be satisfied with the theory.'

'Certainly I shall. If a man like you, who knows the animals from experience, can't hazard a good guess at any rate, who is even to try?'

'Well then, sir, I accounts for it this way: it seems to me that 'ere wolf escaped simply because he wanted to get out.'

From the hearty way that both Thomas and his wife laughed at the joke I could see that it had done service before, and that the whole explanation was simply an elaborate sell. I couldn't cope in badinage with the worthy Thomas, but I thought I knew a surer way to his heart, so I said:-

'Now, Mr Bilder, we'll consider that first half-sovereign worked off, and this brother of his is waiting to be claimed when you've told me what you think will happen.'

'Right y'are, sir,' he said briskly. 'Ye'll excoose me, I know, for a-chaffin' of ye, but the old woman here winked at me, which was as much as telling me to go on.'

'Well, I never!' said the old lady.

'My opinion is this: that 'ere wolf is a-'idin' of, somewheres. The gard'ner wot didn't remember said he was a-gallopin' northward faster than a horse could go; but I don't believe him, for, yer see, sir, wolves don't gallop no more than dogs does, they not bein' built that way. Wolves is fine things in a story-book, and I dessay when they gets in packs and does be chivvin' somethin' that's more afeared than they is they can make a devil of a noise and chop it up, whatever it is. But, Lor' bless you, in real life a wolf is only a low creature, not half so clever as a good dog; and not half a quarter so much fight in 'im. This one ain't been used to fightin' or even to providin' for hisself, and more like he's somewhere round the Park a-'idin' an' a-shiverin' of, and, if he thinks at all, wonderin' where he is to get his breakfast from; or maybe he's got down some area and is in a coal-cellar. My eye, won't some cook get a rum start when she sees his green eyes a-shining at her out of the dark! If he can't get food he's bound to look for it, and mayhap he may chance to light on a butcher's shop in time. If he doesn't, and some nursemaid goes a-walkin' orf with a soldier, leavin' of the hinfant in the perambulator—well then I shouldn't be surprised if the census is one babby the less. That's all.'

I was handing him the half-sovereign, when something came bobbing up against the window, and Mr Bilder's face doubled its natural length with surprise.

'God bless me!' he said. 'If there ain't old Bersicker come back by 'isself!'

He went to the door and opened it; a most unnecessary proceeding it seemed to me. I have always thought that a wild animal never looks so well as when some obstacle of pronounced durability is between us; a personal experience has intensified rather than diminished that idea.

After all, however, there is nothing like custom, for neither Bilder nor his wife thought any more of the wolf than I should of a dog. The animal itself was as peaceful and well-behaved as that father of all picture-wolves, Red Riding Hood's quondam friend, whilst seeking her confidence in masquerade.

The whole scene was an unutterable mixture of comedy and pathos. The wicked wolf that for half a day had paralysed London and set all the children in the town shivering in their shoes, was there in a sort of penitent mood, and was received and petted like a sort of vulpine prodigal son. Old Bilder examined him all over with most tender solicitude, and when he had finished with his penitent said:

'There, I knew the poor old chap would get into some kind of trouble; didn't I say it all along? Here's his head all cut and full of broken glass. 'E's been a-gettin' over some bloomin' wall or other. It's a shyme that people are allowed to top their walls with broken bottles. This 'ere's what comes of it. Come along, Bersicker.'

He took the wolf and locked him up in a cage, with a piece of meat that satisfied, in quantity at any rate, the elementary conditions of the fatted calf, and went off to report.

I came off, too, to report the only exclusive information that is given to-day regarding the strange escapade at the Zoo,

Report from Patrick Hennessey, M.D., M.R.C.S.,
L.K.Q.C.P.I., etc., etc., to John Seward, M.D.

'20 September.

'My dear Sir,—

'In accordance with your wishes, I enclose report of the conditions of everything left in my charge. . . . With regard to patient, Renfield, there is more to say. He has had another outbreak which might have had a dreadful ending, but which, as it fortunately happened, was unattended with any unhappy results. This afternoon a carrier's cart with two men made a call at the empty house whose grounds abut on ours—the house to which, you will remember, the patient twice ran away. The men stopped at our gate to ask the porter their way, as they were strangers. I was myself looking out of the study window, having a smoke after dinner, and saw one of them come up to the house. As he passed the window of Renfield's room, the patient began to rate him from within, and called him all the foul names he could lay his tongue to. The man, who seemed a decent fellow enough, contented himself by telling him to "shut up for a foul-mouthed beggar," whereon our man accused him of robbing him and wanting to murder him and said that he would hinder him if he were to swing for it. I opened the window and signed to the man not to notice, so he contented himself after looking the place over and making up his mind as to what kind of place he had got to by saying: "Lor' bless yer, sir, I wouldn't mind what was said to me in a bloomin' madhouse. I pity ye and the guv'nor for havin' to live in the house with a wild beast like that." Then he asked the way civilly enough, and I told him where the gate of the empty house was; he went away, followed by threats and curses and revilings from our man. I went down to see if I could make out any cause for his anger, since he is usually such a well-behaved man, and except his violent fits nothing of the kind had ever occurred. I found him, to my astonishment, quite composed and most genial in his manner. I tried to get him to talk of the incident, but he blandly asked me questions as to what I meant, and led me to believe that he was completely oblivious of the affair. It was, I am sorry to say, however, only another instance of his cunning, for within half an hour I heard of him again. This time he had broken out through the window of his room, and was running down the avenue. I called to the attendants to follow me, and ran after him, for I feared he was intent on some mischief. My fear was justified when I saw the same cart which had passed before coming down the road, having on it some great wooden boxes. The men were wiping their foreheads, and were flushed in the face, as if with violent exercise. Before I could get up to him the patient rushed at them, and pulling one of them off the cart, began to knock his head against the ground. If I had not seized him just at the moment I believe he would have killed the man there and then. The other fellow jumped down and struck him over the head with the butt-end of his heavy whip. It was a terrible blow; but he did not seem to mind it, but seized him also, and struggled with the three of us, pulling us to and fro as if we were kittens. You know I am no light weight, and the others were both burly men. At first he was silent in his fighting; but as we began to master him, and the attendants were putting a strait-waistcoat on him, he began to shout: "I'll frustrate them! They shan't rob me! they shan't murder me by inches! I'll fight for my Lord and Master!" and all sorts of similar incoherent ravings. It was with very considerable difficulty that they got him back to the house and put him in the padded room. One of the attendants, Hardy, had a finger broken. However, I set it all right; and he is going on well.

'The two carriers were at first loud in their threats of action for damages, and promised to rain all the penalties of the law on us. Their threats were, however, mingled with some sort of indirect apology for the defeat of the two of them by a feeble madman. They said that if it had not been for the way their strength had been spent in carrying and raising the heavy boxes to the cart they would have made short work of him. They gave as another reason for their defeat the extraordinary state of drouth to which they had been reduced by the dusty nature of their occupation and the reprehensible distance from the scene of their labours of any place of public entertainment. I quite understood their drift, and after a stiff glass of grog, or rather more of the same, and with each a sovereign in hand, they made light of the attack, and swore that they would encounter a worse madman any day for the pleasure of meeting so "bloomin' good a bloke" as your correspondent. I took their names and addresses, in case they might be needed. They are as follows:—Jack Smollet, of Dudding's Rents, King George's Road, Great Walworth, and Thomas Snelling, Peter Parley's Row, Guide Court, Bethnal Green. They are both in the employment of Harris & Sons, Moving and Shipment Company, Orange Master's Yard, Soho.

'I shall report to you any matter of interest occurring here, and shall wire you at once if there is anything of importance.

'Believe me, dear Sir,

'Yours faithfully,

'PATRICK HENNESSEY.'

The 'Westminster Gazette', 25 September
Extra Special

THE HAMPSTEAD HORROR
ANOTHER CHILD INJURED
The 'Bloofer Lady'

We have just received intelligence that another child, missed last night, was only discovered late in the morning under a furze bush at the Shooter's Hill side of Hampstead Heath, which is, perhaps, less frequented than the other parts. It has the same tiny wound in the throat as has been noticed in other cases. It was terribly weak, and looked quite emaciated. It too, when partially restored, had the common story to tell of being lured away by the 'bloofer lady.'

DR SEWARD'S DIARY *(continued)*

29 September.—There was a long spell of silence, a big, aching void, and then from the Professor a keen 'S-s-s-s!' He pointed; and far down the avenue of yews we saw a white figure advance—a dim white figure, which held something dark at its breast. The figure stopped, and at the moment a ray of moonlight fell between the masses of driving clouds and showed in startling prominence a dark-haired woman, dressed in the cerements of the grave. We could not see the face, for it was bent down over what we saw to be a fair-haired child. There was a pause and a sharp little cry, such as a child gives in sleep, or a dog as it lies before the fire and dreams. We were starting forward, but the Professor's warning hand, seen by us as he stood behind a yew-tree, kept us back; and then as we looked the white figure moved forward again. It was now near enough for us to see clearly, and the moonlight still held. My own heart grew cold as ice, and I could hear the gasp of Arthur as we recognized the features of Lucy Westenra. Lucy Westenra, but yet how changed. The sweetness was turned to adamantine, heartless cruelty, and the purity to voluptuous wantonness. Van Helsing stepped out, and, obedient to his gesture, we all advanced too; the four of us ranged in a line before the door of the tomb. Van Helsing raised his lantern and drew the slide; by the concentrated light that fell on Lucy's face we could see that the lips were crimson with fresh blood, and that the stream had trickled over her chin and stained the purity of her lawn death-robe.

We shuddered with horror. I could see by the tremulous light that even Van Helsing's iron nerve had failed. Arthur was next to me, and if I had not seized his arm and held him up, he would have fallen.

When Lucy—I call the thing that was before us Lucy because it bore her shape—saw us she drew back with an angry snarl, such as a cat gives when taken unawares; then her eyes ranged over us. Lucy's eyes in form and colour; but Lucy's eyes unclean and full of hell-fire, instead of the pure, gentle orbs we knew. At that moment the remnant of my love passed into hate and loathing; had she then to be killed, I could have done it with savage delight. As she looked, her eyes blazed with unholy light, and the face became wreathed with a voluptuous smile. Oh, God, how it made me shudder to see it! With a careless motion, she flung to the ground, callous as a devil, the child that up to now she had clutched strenuously to her breast, growling over it as a dog growls over a bone. The child gave a sharp cry, and lay there moaning. There was a cold-bloodedness in the act which wrung a groan from Arthur; when she advanced to him with outstretched arms and a wanton smile, he fell back and hid his face in his hands.

She still advanced, however, and with a languorous, voluptuous grace, said:—

'Come to me, Arthur. Leave these others and come to me. My arms are hungry for you. Come, and we can rest together. Come, my husband, come!'

There was something diabolically sweet in her tones—something of the tingling of glass when struck—which rang through the brains even of us who heard the words addressed to another. As for Arthur, he seemed under a spell; moving his hands from his face, he opened wide his arms. She was leaping for them, when Van Helsing sprang forward and held between them his little golden crucifix. She recoiled from it, and, with a suddenly distorted face, full of rage, dashed past him as if to enter the tomb.

When within a foot or two of the door, however, she stopped as if arrested by some irresistible force. Then she turned, and her face was shown in the clear burst of moonlight and by the lamp, which had now no quiver from Van Helsing's iron nerves. Never did I see such baffled malice on a face; and never, I trust, shall such ever be seen again by mortal eyes. The beautiful colour became livid, the eyes seemed to throw out sparks of hell-fire, the brows were wrinkled as though the folds of the flesh were the coils of Medusa's snakes, and the lovely, blood-stained mouth grew to an open square, as in the passion masks of the Greeks and Japanese. If ever a face meant death—if looks could kill—we saw it at that moment.

And so for full half a minute, which seemed an eternity, she remained between the lifted crucifix and the sacred closing of her means of entry. Van Helsing broke the silence by asking Arthur:—

'Answer me, oh my friend! Am I to proceed in my work?'

Arthur threw himself on his knees, and hid his face in his hands, as he answered:—

'Do as you will, friend; do as you will. There can be no horror like this ever any more!' and he groaned in spirit. Quincey and I simultaneously moved towards him, and took his arms. We could hear the click of the closing lantern as Van Helsing held it down; coming close to the tomb, he began to remove from the chinks some of the sacred emblem which he had placed there. We all looked on in horrified amazement as we saw, when he stood back, the woman, with a corporeal body as real at the moment as our own, pass in through the interstice where scarce a knife-blade could have gone. We all felt a glad sense of relief when we saw the Professor calmly restoring the strings of putty to the edges of the door.

MINA HARKER'S JOURNAL

29 September.—After dinner I came with Dr Seward to his study. He brought back the phonograph from my room, and I took my typewriter. He placed me in a comfortable chair, and arranged the phonograph so that I could touch it without getting up, and showed me how to stop it in case I should want to pause. Then he very thoughtfully took a chair, with his back to me, so that I might be as free as possible, and began to read. I put the forked metal to my ears and listened.

When the terrible story of Lucy's death, and—and all that followed, was done, I lay back in my chair powerless. Fortunately I am not of a fainting disposition. When Dr Seward saw me he jumped up with a horrified exclamation, and hurriedly taking a case-bottle from a cupboard, gave me some brandy, which in a few minutes somewhat restored me. My brain was all in a whirl, and only that there came through all the multitude of horrors the holy ray of light that my dear, dear Lucy was at last at peace, I do not think I could have borne it without making a scene. It is all so wild, and mysterious, and strange, that if I had not known Jonathan's experience in Transylvania I could not have believed. As it was, I didn't know what to believe, and so got out of my difficulty by attending to something else. I took the cover off my typewriter, and said to Dr Seward:—

'Let me write this all out now. We must be ready for Dr Van Helsing when he comes. I have sent a telegram to Jonathan to come on here when he arrives in London from Whitby. In this matter dates are everything, and I think if we get all our material ready, and have every item put in chronological order, we shall have done much. You tell me that Lord Godalming and Mr Morris are coming too. Let us be able to tell them when they come.' He accordingly set the phonograph at a slow pace, and I began to typewrite from the beginning of the seventh cylinder. I used manifold, and so took three copies of the diary, just as I had done with all the rest. It was late when I got through, but Dr Seward went about his work of going his round of the patients; when he had finished he came back and sat near me, reading, so that I did not feel too lonely whilst I worked. How good and thoughtful he is; the world seems full of good men—even if there *are* monsters in it. Before I left him I remembered what Jonathan put in his diary of the Professor's perturbation at reading something in an evening paper at the station at Exeter; so, seeing that Dr Seward keeps his newspapers, I borrowed the files of the *Westminster Gazette* and the *Pall Mall Gazette*, and took them to my room. I remember how much the *Dailygraph* and the *Whitby Gazette*, of which I had made cuttings, helped us to understand the terrible events at Whitby when Count Dracula landed, so I shall look through the evening papers since then, and perhaps I shall get some new light. I am not sleepy, and the work will help to keep me quiet.

MINA HARKER'S JOURNAL

1 October.— I can't quite remember how I fell asleep last night. I remember hearing the sudden barking of the dogs and a lot of queer sounds, like braying on a very tumultuous scale, from Mr Renfield's room, which is somewhere under this. And then there was silence over everything, silence so profound that it startled me, and I got up and looked out of the window. All was dark and silent, the black shadows thrown by the moonlight seeming full of a silent mystery of their own. Not a thing seemed to be stirring, but all to be grim and fixed as death or fate; so that a thin streak of white mist, that crept with almost imperceptible slowness across the grass towards the house, seemed to have a sentience and a vitality of its own. I think that the digression of my thoughts must have done me good, for when I got back to bed I found a lethargy creeping over me. I lay awhile, but could not quite sleep, so I got out and looked out of the window again. The mist was spreading, and was now close up to the house, so that I could see it lying thick against the wall, as though it were stealing up to the windows. The poor man was more loud than ever, and though I could not distinguish a word he said, I could in some way recognize in his tones some passionate entreaty on his part. Then there was the sound of a struggle, and I knew that the attendants were dealing with him. I was so frightened that I crept into bed, and pulled the clothes over my head, putting my fingers in my ears. I was not then a bit sleepy, at least so I thought; but I must have fallen asleep, for, except dreams, I do not remember anything until the morning, when Jonathan woke me. I think that it took me an effort and a little time to realize where I was, and that it was Jonathan who was bending over me. My dream was very peculiar, and was almost typical of the way that waking thoughts become merged in, or continued in, dreams.

I thought that I was asleep, and waiting for Jonathan to come back. I was very anxious about him, and I was powerless to act; my feet, and my hands, and my brain were weighted, so that nothing could proceed at the usual pace. And so I slept uneasily and thought. Then it began to dawn upon me that the air was heavy, and dank, and cold. I put back the clothes from my face, and found, to my surprise, that all was dim around me. The gas-light which I had left lit for Jonathan, but turned down, came only like a tiny red spark through the fog, which had evidently grown thicker and poured into the room. Then it occurred to me that I had shut the window before I had come to bed. I would have got out to make certain on the point, but some leaden lethargy seemed to chain my limbs and even my will. I lay still and endured; that was all. I closed my eyes, but could still see through my eyelids. (It is wonderful what tricks our dreams play us, and how conveniently we can imagine.) The mist grew thicker and thicker, and I could see now how it came in, for I could see it like smoke—or with the white energy of boiling water—pouring in, not through the window, but through the joinings of the door. It got thicker and thicker, till it seemed as if it became concentrated into a sort of pillar of cloud in the room, through the top of which I could see the light of the gas shining like a red eye. Things began to whirl through my brain just as the cloudy column was now whirling in the room, and through it all came the scriptural words 'a pillar of cloud by day and of fire by night.' Was it indeed some spiritual guidance that was coming to me in my sleep? But the pillar was composed of both the day and the night guiding, for the fire was in the red eye, which at the thought got a new fascination for me; till, as I looked, the fire divided, and seemed to shine on me through the fog like two red eyes, such as Lucy told me of in her momentary mental wandering when, on the cliff, the dying sunlight struck the windows of St Mary's Church. Suddenly the horror burst upon me that it was thus that Jonathan had seen those awful women growing into reality through the whirling mist in the moonlight, and in my dream I must have fainted, for all became black darkness. The last conscious effort which imagination made was to show me a livid white face bending over me out of the mist. I must be careful of such dreams, for they would unseat one's reason if there was too much of them. I would get Dr Van Helsing or Dr Seward to prescribe something for me which would make me sleep, only that I fear to alarm them. Such a dream at the present time would become woven into their fears for me. To-night I shall strive hard to sleep naturally. If I do not, I shall to-morrow night get them to give me a dose of chloral; that cannot hurt me for once, and it will give me a good night's sleep. Last night tired me more than if I had not slept at all.

DR SEWARD'S PHONOGRAPH DIARY,
SPOKEN BY VAN HELSING

4 October.— This to Jonathan Harker.

You are to stay with your dear Madam Mina. We shall go to make our search—if I can call it so, for it is not search but knowing, and we seek confirmation only. But do you stay and take care of her to-day. This is your best and most holiest office. This day nothing can find him here. Let me tell you that so you will know what we four know already, for I have tell them. He, our enemy, have gone away; he have gone back to his Castle in Transylvania. I know it so well, as if a great hand of fire wrote it on the wall. He have prepared for this in some way, and that last earth-box was ready to ship somewheres. For this he took the money; for this he hurried at the last, lest we catch him before the sun go down. It was his last hope, save that he might hide in the tomb, that he think poor Miss Lucy, being as he thought like him, keep open to him. But there was not of time. When that fail he make straight for his last resource—his last earthwork I might say did I wish *double entente*. He is clever, oh, so clever! he know that his game here was finish; and so he decide he go back home. He find ship going by the route he came, and he go in it. We go off now to find what ship, and wither bound; when we have discovered that, we come back and tell you all. Then we will comfort you and poor dear Madam Mina with new hope. For it will be hope when you think it over: that all is not lost. This very creature that we pursue, he take hundreds of years to get so far as London; and yet in one day, when we know of the disposal of him, we drive him out. He is finite, though he is powerful to do much harm and suffers not as we do. But we are strong, each in our purpose; and we are all more strong together. Take heart afresh, dear husband of Madam Mina. This battle is but begun, and in the end we shall win—so sure as that God sits on high to watch over His children. Therefore be of much comfort till we return.

VAN HELSING

MINA HARKER'S JOURNAL

30 October.—Mr Morris took me to the hotel where our rooms had been ordered by telegraph, he being the one who could best be spared, since he does not speak any foreign language. The forces were distributed much as they had been at Varna, except that Lord Godalming went to the Vice-Consul, as his rank might serve as an immediate guarantee of some sort to the official, we being in extreme hurry. Jonathan and the two doctors went to the shipping agent to learn particulars of the arrival of the *Czarina Catherine*.

Later.—Lord Godalming has returned. The Consul is away, and the Vice-Consul sick; so the routine work has been attended to by a clerk. He was very obliging, and offered to do anything in his power.

MINA HARKER'S JOURNAL

6 November.—In the midst of this I could see that Jonathan on one side of the ring of men, and Quincey on the other, were forcing a way to the cart; it was evident that they were bent on finishing their task before the sun should set. Nothing seemed to stop or even to hinder them. Neither the levelled weapons or the flashing knives of the gipsies in front, or the howling of the wolves behind, appeared to even attract their attention. Jonathan's impetuosity, and the manifest singleness of his purpose, seemed to overawe those in front of him; instinctively they cowered aside and let him pass. In an instant he had jumped upon the cart, and, with a strength which seemed incredible, raised the great box, and flung it over the wheel to the ground. In the meantime, Mr Morris had had to use force to pass through his side of the ring of Szgany. All the time I had been breathlessly watching Jonathan I had, with the tail of my eye, seen him pressing desperately forward, and had seen the knives of the gipsies flash as he won a way through them, and they cut at him. He parried with his great bowie knife, and at first I thought that he too had come through in safety; but as he sprang beside Jonathan, who had by now jumped from the cart, I could see that with his left hand he was clutching at his side, and that the blood was spurting through his fingers. He did not delay notwithstanding this, for as Jonathan, with desperate energy, attacked one end of the chest, attempting to prise off the lid with his great Kukri knife, he attacked the other frantically with his bowie. Under the efforts of both men the lid began to yield; the nails drew with a quick screeching sound, and the top of the box was thrown back.

By this time the gipsies, seeing themselves covered by the Winchesters, and at the mercy of Lord Godalming and Dr Seward, had given in and made no further resistance. The sun was almost down on the mountain tops, and the shadows of the whole group fell long upon the snow. I saw the Count lying within the box upon the earth, some of which the rude falling from the cart had scattered over him. He was deathly pale, just like a waxen image, and the red eyes glared with the horrible vindictive look which I knew too well.

As I looked, the eyes saw the sinking sun, and the look of hate in them turned to triumph.

But, on the instant, came the sweep and flash of Jonathan's great knife. I shrieked as I saw it shear through the throat; whilst at the same moment Mr Morris' bowie knife plunged in the heart.

It was like a miracle; but before our very eyes, and almost in the drawing of a breath, the whole body crumbled into dust and passed from our sight.

I shall be glad as long as I live that even in that moment of final dissolution there was in the face a look of peace, such as I never could have imagined might have rested there.

The Castle of Dracula now stood out against the red sky, and every stone of its broken battlements was articulated against the light of the setting sun.

The gipsies, taking us as in some way the cause of the extraordinary disappearance of the dead man, turned, without a word, and rode away as if for their lives. Those who were unmounted jumped upon the leiter-waggon and shouted to the horsemen not to desert them. The wolves, which had withdrawn to a safe distance, followed in their wake, leaving us alone.

Mr Morris, who had sunk to the ground, leaned on his elbow, holding his hand pressed to his side; the blood still gushed through his fingers. I flew to him, for the Holy circle did not now keep me back; so did the two doctors. Jonathan knelt behind him and the wounded man laid back his head on his shoulder. With a sigh he took, with a feeble effort, my hand in that of his own which was unstained. He must have seen the anguish of my heart in my face, for he smiled at me and said:—

'I am only too happy to have been of any service! Oh, God!' he cried suddenly, struggling up to a sitting posture and pointing to me, 'it was worth this to die! Look! Look!'

The sun was now right down upon the mountain top, and the red gleams fell upon my face, so that it was bathed in rosy light. With one impulse the men sank on their knees, and a deep and earnest 'Amen' broke from all as their eyes followed the pointing of his finger as the dying man spoke:—

'Now God be thanked that all has not been in vain! See! the snow is not more stainless than her forehead! The curse has passed away!'

And, to our bitter grief, with a smile and silence, he died, a gallant gentleman.

VAMPIRES AND AMERICAN ENTHUSIASTS

HOWARD JACKSON

'LEAVE ME ALONE'

'I AM LEGEND'
RICHARD MATHESON

'*I Am Legend*' is to science fiction pulp and to horror what '*The Catcher In The Rye*' is to literature. It confirms to alienated teenagers that the neighbours they resent really are awful. In '*I Am Legend*', the neighbours, the suburban crowd, have become destructive vampires. An apocalypse might make existence more difficult and drain the spirit but motivation is simple. The hero of '*I Am Legend*' has to battle to survive. All the vampires are a threat, the infected and the '*living dead*'. As their prime target, the hero needs to kill as many as he can simply to continue. The final consolation for him is that his stubborn resistance and his unwillingness to join his new community will make his enemies acknowledge him as a legend.

This is an odd fate for a man whose destiny is to live and die alone. Robert Neville, the hero of '*I Am Legend*', is not an extrovert. He only steps outside in the daytime when the vampires are asleep and the streets are deserted. At night, he retreats to his boarded home. He is different from those who are desperate to be noticed, especially the violent narcissists who, to achieve momentary fame, are willing to sacrifice not only their own lives but also the lives of those within their own community. We have witnessed and now understand how dark adolescent fantasies can produce horror and not merely romantic heroism. Fans are biased, so I am reluctant to believe that the novel by Matheson has contributed to the suburban slayings that exist in the modern world, especially those in the United States. But I remember reading warily the account of the Columbine slaughter. I hoped that there would be no mention of '*I Am Legend*' and I was relieved to discover that the killers were inspired by darker and inferior material. Fiction, of course, only makes a modest contribution to the motives of a mass murderer who has compulsions more powerful than the inspiration found in a book.

Escapist art may offer relief to the tormented and possibly inspire individuals to be violent in specific moments but it is not likely to persuade someone to become a mass murderer and take wholesale action. Richard Neville is a determined stubborn character but he only begins to kill his neighbours after they become vampires.

Readers like and can identify with the hero of 'I Am Legend'. Yet every day when there is sunlight, this sympathetic figure seeks and murders his neighbours. The author is reticent about the number of killings but one day he actually mentions the total. On the day quoted and in less than 12 hours, Robert Neville killed 47 of the local population. (IAL,16) Neville survives for 3 years and murders most days. The only exceptions are the cloudy days during which he stays indoors. He does this to avoid the sunset and escape the vampires emerging from sleep. The mathematics is obvious. Robert Neville, a man who was once happy to work, talk sport with his neighbour, Ben Cortman, and watch his family grow, murders thousands.

It feels strange to mention mass murderers in the context of 'I Am Legend'. Robert Neville is a resolute hero sustaining the good fight against evil. In 'I Am Legend', he is the only hope against the apocalypse or so it seems for most of the book. We want him to prevail.

Matheson based the character of Neville on Robinson Crusoe, and there is actually a reference to Crusoe in 'I Am Legend'. Robert Neville compares himself to the Defoe hero. 'No longer will you be a weird Robinson Crusoe, imprisoned on an island of night surrounded by oceans of death.' (IAL,73) The sentence is not only over-written, a rare exception in 'I Am Legend', it is not necessary. Long before page 73 of the book, the reader has realised that Matheson has used the vampire myth to create a weird modern paranoid version of 'Robinson Crusoe'.

The introduction to the Wordsworth edition of the novel by Defoe states that 'there is still a strong Robinson Crusoe echo in numerous science fiction films, such as 'The Omega Man'(W,X1). The novel 'I Am Legend' is not mentioned which is disappointing especially as the film quoted is an inadequate adaptation of the book. But this can be forgiven because the author of the introduction,

Doreen Roberts, understands that the neighbours are both *'agents of evil'* and *'innocent victims'*. Roberts also describes the film hero as *'an apostle of the gun'*. Not every reader of *'I Am Legend'* will think of the hero of the book in this way. It probably requires the realism of film to appreciate completely the violent implications within the book.

For most, Neville is a modern Crusoe intent on survival rather than destruction. The plot alone makes it clear that the Defoe novel inspired Matheson. The various references include the dog, the footprint that Crusoe discovers, the encounter with Friday, the emphasis on practical ability and a dedicated hero who will take time and expend effort to understand his environment and construct tools for survival. Although some of these comparisons are inverted, for example the footprint is now a germ on the slide of a microscope, the book clearly exists as a tribute to an earlier work. Of course, Robert Neville is an American hero so it is no surprise that he is willing to use his gun and weapons. The island has become the frontier with a solitary pioneer resolved to fight hostile natives. Defoe imagines the lone individual creating agriculture. Matheson imagines an urban scavenging mountain man inside a fort. This is what is left of the suburb, his solitary house. The other houses have been burnt down by Neville to prevent the vampires leaping on to his roof.

Not only is the original Robinson Crusoe well known but, like the vampire, the solitary island dweller has had many incarnations, sometimes comic. The existence of the comic versions confirms what we know, that the idea of being perpetually alone makes us uneasy. We need to poke fun and laugh. One comic version has stayed in my mind and it worried me well before I was familiar with either *'Robinson Crusoe'* or *'I Am Legend'*.

These days the reputation of the comedian Benny Hill has suffered. He is regarded as crude and sexist. Admittedly, he always had a fondness for titillation and had no scruples in adding pretty girls to his sketches but the comic who worked for the BBC was less obvious and crude than the reinvention that appeared later on ITV. One of his sketches has haunted me all my life. This is how I remember it.

Benny is in a spaceship. They have landed on a planet that has toxic air that shrinks people so they are no taller than four inches. The three female members of the crew who are all attractive have stepped outside and been shrunken. Benny and the co-pilot are still inside the space ship. One of the walls of the space ship is supposedly made of magnifying glass that makes the women appear normal size. The women constantly plead with Benny to join them outside. Much of the sketch is Benny working hard to prevent his co-pilot from joining the women. Eventually, the co-pilot relents and Benny loses his temper. He throws a beer bottle out of the spaceship and at his tormentors. Now he has four people to torment him. The beer bottle, of course, looks enormous. Everybody other than Benny prepares for a party. Soon, Benny is tricked to stepping outside. Hill is a cynic so it is no surprise that the scene finishes with a happy space captain drinking beer and surrounded by accommodating females.

Why did a silly sketch torment me for so long? Well, the women were attractive. But something else nagged, something that was probably beyond the understanding of the child that watched the TV. Even without reading 'I Am Legend', I felt that nobody should be obliged to make the decision that faced poor Benny. My guess is that what stuck inside my head was the irrevocability or the consequence of the decision. Once he stepped outside, he would always be four inches tall but if he stayed inside he would forfeit everything that the women and his friend offered, company and gratification. I have no illusions about the 'magnifying' window. This was an idea necessitated by cheap BBC special effects but the existence of women who appeared to be normal size also exaggerated the temptation so it became irresistible and real. Hill had to endure the choice that we all face, persistence or surrender.

Did Benny Hill think of his sketch after reading 'I Am Legend'? I like to think so but who knows. The creation by Hill relates more to the novel by Matheson than the book by Defoe. Crusoe does not have to resist temptation from others whereas the vampires taunt Robert Neville nightly. As their behaviour makes clear, he is alone and they have friends. The Benny Hill sketch is concerned with what later appeared to be a personal obsession, sexual temptation, and how, as Oscar Wilde warned, resistance is beyond us. Temptation features in '*I Am Legend*' although it is not sexual. Neville conquers his desires by averting his eyes from the female vampires. The temptation he has to endure is the daily desire to relent and relax. His efforts require a will to persist, and he works and strives to ensure survival. '*Robinson Crusoe*' and '*I Am Legend*' have heroes determined by fate, and both have to accept that fate to survive. Crusoe calls it providence, and it is his acceptance of providence that helps him to understand and accept God. He becomes a religious man. Neville is not religious. At one point he says, '*If I were religious now*' (87). He does not ponder why he is the only man that has survived, neither as a religious nor an existential question. He thinks it is an accident of immunity, determined by a bite from a bat that occurred before the apocalypse. Later, when he meets the woman, Ruth, the Friday equivalent in '*I Am Legend*', she asks the question, '*Why are we still alive? Why aren't we all dead?*'(139). Neville instead says, '*It just is.* (139)'

'*I Am Legend*' like '*Robinson Crusoe*' is a fatalistic work. Either God or fate defines our futures. What both books do, though, is insist that effort and willpower are important, even though the consequences are determined elsewhere. Effort and will alone do not determine the future because fortuitous accidents and events need to happen. Fate needs help. This is why the search for knowledge is important. Continuous enquiry makes the accidents consequential but never in a way that can be predicted by the curious and industrious who unwittingly create the accidents.

In '*Robinson Crusoe*,' the future is the will of God but because of the impact of unintended consequences the efforts of Crusoe exist as a metaphor for the progress of the human race. Progress is never what the hapless human imagines but through accident, determination and fortune humans do develop. Defoe, though, creates a powerful and admirable hero who undermines his argument. For all his self-effacing insistence on providence, the actions of Crusoe demonstrate that effort is important and the future is not merely the will of God.

Yet, in *'Robinson Crusoe'*, we have a hero who believes in *'the wisdom of providence'*, and in *'I Am Legend'*, Robert Matheson has created someone who accepts he will be unable to alter fate. Certainly, Neville wants to discover the scientific explanation behind the existence of vampires. But he does not believe his efforts will alter his ultimate destiny although they may prolong his life and help him add to the body count. His research is driven by a curiosity inspired by the presence of the vampires on his lawns. Both Crusoe and Neville work hard and are relentless in their efforts. The two books, though, have a fatalism that challenges modern notions of hard working individualism. Even Robinson Crusoe, who prospers, only leaves the island after an unscheduled arrival of a Spanish ship.

If the two heroes have recognizable imperialist traits, it is because they are products of their society. Crusoe is a shipwrecked English sailor, and Neville is an American with wartime experience. They carry guns and know how to plunder. Neither, though, is creating a new world. They make their environments as habitable as they can be but without the prospect of civilisation. If Crusoe helps us to realise how the human race adapted and prospered, it is an indirect metaphor rather than the theme of the book, which is much more explicit about the wisdom of religious faith. Neville has no prospects of a new world, his activity is limited to efficient scavenging and slaughter. The notion of a new world only emerges later when we again meet Ruth, the woman that Neville previously found and captured like Crusoe did his Friday. She has returned to tell Neville that the infected are creating a new society and are killing the *'living dead'*. Crusoe threw away corn that grew into a crop. The infected have discovered that they can build up a resistance to the sun. Accidents determine the future, which is why our existence is always undermined by irony.

Despite that understanding, both *'Crusoe'* and *'Legend'* are moral books. Both insist upon a work ethic and argue that effort is consequential despite the independence of fate. Extreme circumstances, such as the desert island where Crusoe has to make his home or the vampire apocalypse that Neville has to accept, help us understand the true purpose of puritanical will. Work and more importantly self-discipline convince us that we cannot only prevail but also endure less unpleasantly. We need to work to create comfort.

Throughout the book, Neville has complicated feelings towards the infected. He wants to kill them but is prepared to invite a diseased dog and an infected woman to share his life. The episode with the dog is sentimental but the sentiment is deliberate. Neville wants someone to talk to and he enjoys seeing a creature with a pair of eyes that registers feeling. It is no substitute for human kinship but Neville responds as if it might be. We are not surprised when the dog dies and realism exists again. This is a weak moment for Neville, and it compares to Crusoe who after seeing the footprint, and instead of being pleased by the prospect of human company, spends the next two years in a paranoid hell worrying about threats that only exist in his imagination. These are examples of Crusoe and Neville being human. No life is perfect and, while being alone helps them develop strength, neither man can overcome the fear and the temptation of company. Both have moments when they withdraw from others. After discovering the footprint, Crusoe goes into hiding, and Neville when he hears vampires screams, *'Leave me alone, leave me alone.'*(p8) Crusoe is frightened of strangers he does not know and Neville, like Benny Hill, is frightened of creatures that offer fun but insist on his transformation.

Crusoe is lucky because he finds Friday who becomes a loyal friend. Ruth helps and betrays Neville simultaneously. She warns him so he might be able to escape but she also acts as a spy for the rest of the infected. She has a higher cause than her love or sympathy for Neville. Perhaps the relationship has limited potential. They are different characters. Neville is the man who achieves most alone, through reading books and experiments in his workshop. Ruth is a social animal who educates herself through opportunism. She picks the brains of others to see what they have learnt through their enquiries and their mistakes or 'accidents'. She is a spy and a woman who is not prepared to trust fate. Ruth will play a part in creating the new society and she compares herself to a revolutionary. Neville may feel kinship for Ruth, they like to stand and hold one another quietly, but his humanity is revealed more when he sees the revolutionaries kill his neighbour, Ben Cortman. He is the vampire that Neville has hunted with the intention of killing for three years. Neville hates to see his old friend murdered in the name of progress, even if the old friend taunted him more than anyone. This is a powerful and surprising scene. The savagery of the assassins disgusts Neville but the reader also senses the regret of Neville. The man who has been killed is not only someone who was once an intimate friend. After the apocalypse, Cortman became the worthy foe that Neville will now miss. All this is credible because Neville earlier in the book thinks about the vampires in the same way that Crusoe does about cannibals. They cannot be condemned for ways that are normal to them.

More complicated is why Neville refuses the chance to escape. His reasons for staying and facing his executioners are never properly explained. At one point he says, *'habit keeps me in the house'* (155) but later he reveals that a couple of times he had set out to escape to the mountains but decided against leaving. The suburban 'mountain man' does not want to go to the mountains and face the natural alternative. But he even concedes that he has been stupid and should have gone. We are obliged to interpret the explanation of a man who is incapable of explaining. My view is that Neville needs the vampires as enemies. Without them, there is no threat to resist or no mystery to explain, no reason for existence. The vampires also require a monster and, because of that need, Neville will be remembered as legend. Of course, by refusing to move from his home, Neville finally challenges fate in a world where fate is unavoidable. It is a form of suicide, the only alternative to fate.

In the same introduction to the Wordsworth edition of *'Robinson Crusoe'*, Doreen Roberts identifies five books from English writers that have acquired *'quasi-mythological status'*. These are *'Robinson Crusoe'*, *'Gulliver's Travels'*, *'Alice In Wonderland'*, *'Dracula'* and *'Frankenstein'* although she believes the last two have only acquired that status because of the impact of cinema. '*I Am Legend*' takes the myths from two of the five novels that are viewed as having powerful mythological properties, '*Dracula*' and '*Robinson Crusoe*'. There are different opinions as to whether the themes of these two novels combined easily or whether it required consummate skill by Matheson. What is apparent, though, is that Matheson decided to merge an obvious fantasy and an early serious attempt at realism. Indeed, without any sense of responsibility, Defoe at the beginning of his book describes what follows as a true account. The Cohen Brothers used the same deceit for their film, '*Fargo*'. If the only mixing attempted by Matheson had been fantasy and realism, he would have produced something exceptional. But he also signposts recognized genres so we have science fiction, the book is set in the near future, and gothic horror, the novel includes the icons of vampire fiction. Somewhat like Defoe insisting in his introduction to '*Robinson Crusoe*' that we believe his story to be true, Matheson proclaims that the superstitious rituals with garlic and wooden stakes are rooted in scientific fact. The merging of genres by Matheson enables the book to anticipate the zombie films that are popular today. Zombies are no more than a tribe of vampires who have won or appear to be winning. Clearly, combining gothic and science fiction has potency because '*I Am Legend*' has left a legacy that consists of the alternative zombie tradition. The science fiction genre is also a suitable place to resurrect '*Robinson Crusoe*'. It attracts authors, like Defoe, who have other lives besides literature, practical men with scientific knowledge.

Not only does the amalgamation of genres make the novel feel ironical even when it is merely descriptive, for example when the vampires are taunting Neville from his suburban lawn, it ensures that the intended irony when it is delivered in the climax will feel profound and have mythological consequence. Different readers will respond in different ways. Some will be moved by the realisation that Neville has become the marauding monster and his own double, the one that the others need to destroy and the enemy that they detest yet admire. Others will glory in his unpredicted immortality.

The ending is powerful and it insists upon the importance of gothic memory. Gothic myth depends on something beyond material and scientific fact. At the end of '*I Am Legend*', we understand why. Our illusions and accidental progress will always mean that we misinterpret history and our circumstances. We too easily ignore what exists in the shadows, the forgotten accidents and the important but barely known men and women.

The ending is not religious. Admittedly, there is revelation and redemption. Neville realises that he is the monster but he chuckles when he understands that he has become a legend. For him, there is an afterlife. But Neville does not die closer to God, and there is nothing in the book that suggests that the people in the new society will eventually regret their sacrifice of Neville and transform him into a Christ like figure that will be worshipped. No, Robert Neville will exist as a myth for the future, the last of the suburban men. It will be forgotten that he merely survived because he was blessed with random immunity and survival skills. Instead, the infected will remember a creature with special powers.

The truth will be neglected. Before the vampires, Richard Neville had neighbours and was ordinary. After the vampires appeared, he was alone. He needed fortitude and to make important discoveries. Some men can be valiant but heroes need enemies more than anything. This is perhaps a plain truth with obvious implications, a horrible formula that has led so often to meaningless conflict and violence. The belief that inventing and killing enemies will endow the alienated with heroism has convinced more than one teenage mass murderer. It is why '*I Am Legend*' disturbs as much as it inspires. Even when measured against the standards of dystopian science fiction and gothic horror, this is a book with dark warnings that make it exceptional.

Note

References in parenthesis that begin IAL, refer to Matheson, Richard '*I Am Legend*', (Gollancz Press, 2011)

References that begin W, refer to the introduction of '*Robinson Crusoe*', (Wordsworth Classics, Edition 2000)

LEARNING TO SEE

'FRIGHT NIGHT' – THE ORIGINAL 1985 VERSION

'*We are right back where we started*,' says the voice on the TV in the final scene of the film, '*Fright Night*'. It almost evokes the ending of '*Dracula*' by Bram Stoker where the four heroes fight a monster from the past so that they can keep the future at bay. '*Fright Night*', though, concerns an American adolescent who when he defeats the vampire will survive to become an adult. His victory will ensure a different future, and he will accept the inevitable change of ageing. The plot of the movie requires a likeable hero who may or may not cope with his rites of passage. He needs to replace his absent father, escape his deluded mother, earn the love of his girlfriend and cope with the attentive TV in the corner. He will do that by learning to see properly.

The American TV series, '*Dark Shadows*', had two existences. It ran from 1966 to 1971 for 1225 episodes. A second series appeared twenty years later but this, despite having an accomplished cast, lasted a mere 12 episodes. There is little evidence to suggest that '*Dark Shadows*' inspired the film, '*Fright Night*', but there is a link. The title, '*Fright Night*', refers to the favourite television series of Charlie Brewster, the hero of the film. It is a programme about a vampire killer called Peter Vincent. The name is a tribute to the cinema actors, Peter Cushing and Vincent Price. But '*Dark Shadows*' cannot be ignored. This daytime soap opera was a huge success in the 1960s and a key element in the grooming of American children. The name, Peter Vincent, may have been inspired by cinema greats but the movie, '*Fright Night*', is more concerned with the TV in the corner than Hammer Horror.

'*Fright Night*' is a low budget movie. The success that followed its release was something of a surprise. It led to two remakes, both inferior. The original may be thematic but it never takes itself too seriously. The humour is important and although there are wry moments, like Jerry the vampire humming *'Strangers In The Night'*, it is likeable rather than hilarious.

The movie begins with a camera tracking through an American suburb. The words we hear are sinister. It sounds like an innocent woman being prepared for seduction or something worse. The camera leads us into the bedroom of Charlie Brewster. He is on the floor at the side of the bed attempting to seduce his girlfriend, Amy. Why are they on the floor? Well, things can happen on a bed which is why Amy thinks the floor is safer but interestingly it is also where Charlie cannot see or be seen by the TV. Charlie is not just a looker. His imagination is his strength because it helps him have purpose and know the difference between right and wrong. He will take action when required. But because Charlie has been groomed by the TV in his room he too easily believes what he sees. He thinks the pretend heroes are real so it is likely that he is on the floor with Amy because he does not want his hero, Peter Vincent, to watch him have or fail to have sex with Amy. When Amy relents and climbs on to the bed Charlie is distracted by the sight of a coffin being carried by the new neighbours into the house next door. Like James Stewart in the Hitchcock classic, *'Rear Window'*, Charlie pulls out his binoculars. Amy loses her temper and leaves but not before Charlie and Amy are summoned by his mother. She is also watching the TV. In this household, the television is both the missing father and husband. Later, the suspicions of Charlie increase when again at night, like a popcorn eating James Stewart, he hears a scream from the house next door.

The mother dismisses Charlie's suspicion but she will never learn to see, and it is not too long before she is discharged to the night shift in the local hospital. *'Fright Night'* is a vampire movie written and directed by a man, Tom Holland. The mother is important but she is inadequate. She thinks Jerry the vampire next door is a perfect neighbour and unwittingly invites him into the house. It is the mother that introduces Charlie to the potential elder brother that Charlie has to destroy. Indeed, in their first confrontation, Jerry warns Charlie, like elder brothers have been doing through generations, that he can destroy the mother. The true nature of their confrontation is revealed by what happens to the photograph of Amy. It falls out of the window and on to a stake in the white fence. Later, Charlie will fight to save Amy but this first battle between the two 'brothers' has the younger brother needing to protect the mother. '*And I'd have to kill her, too,*' warns Jerry. Not only has the elder brother sharp dangerous teeth, he has a tongue that can reveal to his mother what the younger son fears most of all, the truth about his voyeuristic self. Undoubtedly, some people who watch '*Fright Night*' will conclude that Jerry is the older father figure that has to be destroyed. But we should not ignore that Bram Stoker based the character '*Dracula*' on the actor, Sir Henry Irving, who both employed and dominated Stoker. So, Peter Vincent may be a reference to Bram Stoker and his substitute father. The existence and subsequent importance of an ageing actor, Peter Vincent, to the destruction of the vampire contradicts the notion of Jerry as a father figure. Charlie is successful in overcoming Jerry because he has the help of Vincent and because he now has a 'father' that is human and because he no longer has to rely on the TV in the corner of the room. In the initial struggle between Jerry and Charlie, Jerry makes the reasonable plea, '*I can give you something that I never had. I can give you a choice. Forget about me and I'll forget about you.*' This is no more than the elder brother asking to be left alone by the younger pest. Jerry reacts with a temper when provoked but left alone he is like most elder brothers. He restricts himself to a superior smirk and veiled threats. He also has the power of all older brothers. He can seduce the younger with friendship. He says to Evil Ed, who is a friend of Charlie, '*I know what it's like being different. All you have to do is take my hand.*'

Perhaps it is the success of Chris Sarandon in the role of the vampire that suggests an older brother. He is a remarkably handsome 43 year-old male and he has all the traits of the elder brother. Jerry has money, the loyal but irritating mate, a superior sound system, the better car, flash clothes and confidence with women. When Amy meets Jerry she describes him as '*real neat*'. After they have realised that Jerry is a vampire, Amy and Charlie, pursued by Jerry, retreat to the local discotheque. The castle owned by Dracula was a place of dread for Jonathan Harker, and the discotheque evokes similar anxieties in young men. Obliged to visit discotheques in pursuit of sex, the young male is enticed into the one location where his entitlement to male power and hierarchy is denied. Instead, rejection and humiliation by women has to be endured. Of course, it is different for men who have money and power. This is why, in the discotheque, Charlie is easily humiliated by Jerry and an easily tempted Amy.

If the myopia of the mother only helps Charlie to hide his voyeuristic nature, neither is Amy, the girlfriend of Charlie, a new woman. True, she takes the initiative in persuading Peter Vincent to reconsider his rejection of Charlie. After her plea and offer of money, Vincent becomes involved in helping the disturbed young man who believes in vampires. Amy, though, does not recruit Vincent to fight Jerry the vampire as Charlie had originally intended. With the help of a giggling and delighted Evil Ed, she concocts a scheme to deceive Charlie. This will be a charade with fake holy water that will prove wrongly that Jerry is not a vampire. Amy is not interested in helping Charlie see properly. She does understand the difference between the reality and the imagination but Amy is too pragmatic to be curious. In 'Fright Night', the woman is quite willing to manipulate what can be seen and exploit the limitations of the male. Few vampire movies are feminist and 'Fright Night' is no exception. Amy exists in order to be rescued and preserved. None of the heroes are women. The women are either uncomprehending mothers or beautiful prostitutes or a girl whose future will be determined exclusively by men. In its attitude to women, it echoes the original novel by Bram Stoker. Only a brave fool would deny the misogyny, and I am not brave, but the hatred of women in 'Fright Night' is also a reflection of fears about inadequate male decency. Charlie imagines a woman like himself, somebody who wants a decent partner to help build a future and provide nurture for the children, someone who can be loved. But when Charlie sees Amy vamped into someone that resembles the girls who visit Jerry, we suspect that Charlie is afraid that

Amy has his own weakness, that she is unable to resist the sex object who offers ecstasy just like he could not when he saw the glamorous blonde prostitute next door. Indeed, when Amy, like Lucy in the novel by Stoker, becomes more forward and suddenly acquires great make up and hair, Charlie is even tempted. The monster that emerges within seconds is a warning what life will be like with a demanding uncontrollable fantasy. Francis Ford Coppola directed a version of *'Dracula'* that was sympathetic to the vampire. Although he denies it, Coppola is believed to have had a relationship with a porn star prior to him making the film, *'Bram Stoker's Dracula'*, and seriously considered casting her as Lucy in his movie.

The interchangeability of men and women is emphasized in the memorable scene where Jerry seduces Amy. Jerry is naked to the waist while Amy wears a backless dress. The male vampire is the object of desire. Unlike in most vampire movies, little emphasis is given to the fangs piercing the neck. Instead, we see three lines of blood run the length of the back of Amy. It suggests the breaking of the hymen but it is also a reminder that in the seduction by the vampire it is the woman who leaves fluid in the body of the man.

In a similar way, roles are reversed between Charlie and his mother. Like Charlie, his mother cannot convince others in conversation, and neither Charlie nor his mother can see properly. His mother sleeps at night with a visor over her eyes. She not only misunderstands the conversations that exist around her but also fails to notice the veiled threats that Jerry the vampire makes against Charlie, her son. Meanwhile, the son believes that everything he sees on the TV is true. This is why he asks an actor, Peter Vincent, to help him destroy Jerry the vampire. When the glamorous blonde visits Jerry next door Charlie is delighted and bounds into his house. We imagine him eagerly searching for his binoculars. The woman he sees is a prostitute but Charlie only realises this when he hears news of her murder on the TV. Before that, she had represented sexual fantasy. Charlie has his suspicions about Jerry confirmed when he watches through the window Jerry seduce the second woman that visits him. Her breasts are exposed, and Charlie is unable to resist staring. Jerry notices and, like the husband in the honeymoon couple in *'Rear Window'*, he pulls down the blind. As the final moment of the film will confirm when we hear against logic the voice of the destroyed Evil Ed, there will always be something that is not seen. The people who can see properly do not see everything. They merely understand properly what they do see. The notion of needing to see properly is emphasized by the character of Evil Ed, the friend of Charlie. Evil is a far less offensive adolescent than his name suggests but he is flawed and exists as the opposite of Charlie. Ed is better at trigonometry than Charlie. Evil Ed can collect knowledge but is perhaps best with symbols and data rather than human reality. Whereas Charlie thinks everything is real including hammy TV programmes about the supernatural, Evil Ed sees everything as if it is all TV entertainment. The film itself uses occasional TV clips and news items to help advance the narrative so we have some sympathy for Evil Ed and Charlie. There is little difference between reality and the imagined on the television. It is all delivered by adult talking heads. Evil Ed giggles at everything including news of the decapitation of the first two victims of Jerry the vampire. Why not? He saw it on the TV. Evil Ed will soon become a victim of Jerry. Charlie may have to understand that Peter Vincent is only an actor but at least he has faith in himself and his own optimism. Lacking faith of any kind, Evil Ed is destined to giggle uncomfortably with terrible pointed teeth and eventually die, killed inevitably by Peter Vincent who has abandoned his role in the imaginary to deal with the real.

When Amy asks Vincent for help the actor imagines that the task will be accomplished with a typical hammy performance. Vincent accepts because he has just been fired and needs money. The ruse designed by Amy is successful but as they are leaving Vincent opens his cigarette case and observes that Jerry has no reflection. This moment of seeing is important to both the theme of the film and the moral progress of Peter Vincent. Despite the presence of vampires, *'Fright Night'* is a feel good comic film. Yet the director, Tom Holland, risks destroying the mood with three graphic scenes involving death and transformation. Peter Vincent witnesses these events and the camera cuts between the grotesque and his shocked incredulous stare, which never wavers. By refusing to avert his eyes, Peter Vincent acquires, despite his cowardly nature, courage and strength. He is now able to witness real horror and not merely fake a pretend substitute. Without this ability, real purpose is impossible. Faith is important in *'Fright Night'* but it is not religious faith. Instead, it is a certainty based on understanding and a confidence in knowledge. Once he can see properly, Peter Vincent can trust the power of the cross. The first task for Vincent and Charlie is to kill Billy Cole who is the servant and friend of Jerry the vampire. This is difficult because the smoke of the gun makes it difficult for Vincent and Charlie to see Cole and aim. Later, after making the effort to see through the smoke, they will be more adept at killing Jerry. Charlie and Vincent will destroy Jerry by smashing the windows of his basement retreat. It not only exposes Jerry to the sunlight but also provides Charlie and Vincent with the light that helps them utilise their improved ability to see. Not surprisingly, there is no TV in the basement.

The movie ends as it begins with a tracking shot that finishes in the bedroom of Charlie. The suburb does not exist at night in silence but has the TV always talking, always in some home persuading somebody somewhere. Vincent has now been reinstated on the TV programme, *'Fright Night'*. Everything is the same as at the beginning except Charlie and Amy are now on the bed and, in his introduction to the episode, Vincent acknowledges Charlie. He has learnt to see as did Charlie but the hello to Charlie that Vincent makes from the TV screen is not just about the two heroes being able to see one another properly. Vincent has become something like a real father. Before the adventure with Jerry the vampire, Charlie only had a box of technology for a friend, a box that was deceitful and stopped Charlie from seeing properly. With the help of his new father, the real Peter Vincent, Charlie can distinguish between reality and imagination. On the TV, Vincent mentions Charlie in the introduction to that night's episode. His acquired son smiles at the TV screen and grins. Secure that he will have the support and approval of a father in the future, he will consummate his relationship with his future wife. Charlie switches off the TV.

The notion of the TV as the surrogate father for American children is not novel. The relationship between son and father dominates American culture. The examples of inadequate sons and overbearing fathers are that many they do not need to be repeated. The strong patriarch is criticized in Westerns like '*The Big Country*' and the male that is dominated by the mother is treated with contempt in teenage angst movies like '*Rebel Without A Cause*'. It may not end there. The heroes of 'Star Wars' are children inside the bodies of adults. This father-fixated film offers a home to the best of American children. They are those who are free of a prejudice and are willing to share a spaceship with a seven feet dog but also those who more importantly refuse to stay on the rug watching the TV. Charlie is a man of action and, as in '*Star Wars*', the male author imagines adolescents being successful where adults have failed. Jerry deals easily with the bouncers with excess muscle who ask him to leave. Faced with a situation that is genuinely difficult, the first bouncer, who looks intimidating, can only shout for a bigger bouncer who is also easily vanquished. The child who watches the TV has no faith in the local heroes and the world of adults. Charlie is fearful but always willing to face Jerry the vampire although he does realise after his first confrontation with Jerry that he needs the help of a father if he is to survive and thwart the threat made against his mother and girlfriend. In a world of inadequate real men and of absent fathers, he seeks help from the television. But if Charlie thinks he is rejecting reality for '*Star Wars*' adolescent fantasy he is mistaken. He will soon learn the truth about Peter Vincent. More worrying, because of the importance of the TV in his home, he is asking the one man whose gaze Charlie tries to avoid when he attempts to seduce Amy. Once he has defeated the vampire, he not only has an approving father but is also able to cope with the critical gaze from the TV. Charlie has achieved this despite living in a house with the number 101 which represents the inadequate nuclear family inside, the mother and son and no father.

Although *'Fright Night'* is primarily concerned with how the integrity of the voyeur is important to moral development, like all vampire movies, it does not neglect identity. Sometimes a different identity emerges because of the vampire bite. For example, Evil Ed becomes more camp. But all the characters, whether bitten or not, have alternative identities. The actress, Amanda Bearse, was picked to play Amy because she has the ability to appear both homely and attractive. The mother of Charlie is not only unable to see but has nightmares about being seen naked yet she can still contribute a worthwhile shift at the local hospital. Charlie is the seedy voyeur but hero. Ed is clever albeit shallow and although irresponsible he is a potentially decent friend. The greatest enigmas are the mature men that are beyond the understanding of the adolescent. The policeman that Charlie engages to help presents adult authority with Charlie but is a submissive juvenile with Billy Cole. Jerry is charming and considerate until angered, and Peter Vincent is a hero except it takes Charlie and others to help him realise his potential. Hammy TV programmes, though, only offer stereotypes of villains and heroes. No wonder Charlie needs to learn to see properly.

Ultimately, the film is positive. It argues that we need not look away from the complex or even the horror. We should not be afraid. The horror that is seen will not diminish those who gaze but what they see will make them strong and help them discover that they too have value and potential. I suppose it is why *'Fright Night'* warrants being called a feel good movie. Or, in the final words of Evil Ed from the unseen dark, *'Oh, you're so cool, Brewster.'*

DRACULA'S GUEST

BRAM STOKER

DRACULA'S GUEST

WHEN we started for our drive the sun was shining brightly on Munich, and the air was full of the joyousness of early summer. Just as we were about to depart, Herr Delbrück (the maître d'hôtel of the Quatre Saisons, where I was staying) came down, bareheaded, to the carriage and, after wishing me a pleasant drive, said to the coachman, still holding his hand on the handle of the carriage door:

'Remember you are back by nightfall. The sky looks bright but there is a shiver in the north wind that says there may be a sudden storm. But I am sure you will not be late.' Here he smiled, and added, 'for you know what night it is.'

Johann answered with an emphatic, 'Ja, mein Herr,' and, touching his hat, drove off quickly. When we had cleared the town, I said, after signalling him to stop:

'Tell me, Johann, what is tonight?'

He crossed himself, as he answered laconically: 'Walpurgis Nacht.' Then he took out his watch, a great, old-fashioned German silver thing as big as a turnip, and looked at it, with his eyebrows gathered together and a little impatient shrug of his shoulders. I realised that this was his way of respectfully protesting against the unnecessary delay, and sank back in the carriage, merely motioning him to proceed. He started off rapidly, as if to make up for lost time. Every now and then the horses seemed to throw up their heads and sniffed the air suspiciously. On such occasions I often looked around in alarm. The road was pretty bleak, for we were traversing a sort of high, wind-swept plateau. As we drove, I saw a road that looked but little used, and which seemed to dip through a little, winding valley. It looked so inviting that, even at the risk of offending him, I called Johann to stop—and when he had pulled up, I told him I would like to drive down that road. He made all sorts of excuses, and frequently crossed himself as he spoke. This somewhat piqued my curiosity, so I asked him various questions. He answered fencingly, and repeatedly looked at his watch in protest. Finally I said:

'Well, Johann, I want to go down this road. I shall not ask you to come unless you like; but tell me why you do not like to go, that is all I ask.' For answer he seemed to throw himself off the box, so quickly did he reach the ground. Then he stretched out his hands appealingly to me, and implored me not to go. There was just enough of English mixed with the German for me to understand the drift of his talk. He seemed always just about to tell me something—the very idea of which evidently frightened him; but each time he pulled himself up, saying, as he crossed himself: 'Walpurgis Nacht!'

I tried to argue with him, but it was difficult to argue with a man when I did not know his language. The advantage certainly rested with him, for although he began to speak in English, of a very crude and broken kind, he always got excited and broke into his native tongue—and every time he did so, he looked at his watch. Then the horses became restless and sniffed the air. At this he grew very pale, and, looking around in a frightened way, he suddenly jumped forward, took them by the bridles and led them on some twenty feet. I followed, and asked why he had done this. For answer he crossed himself, pointed to the spot we had left and drew his carriage in the direction of the other road, indicating a cross, and said, first in German, then in English: 'Buried him—him what killed themselves.'

I remembered the old custom of burying suicides at cross-roads: 'Ah! I see, a suicide. How interesting!' But for the life of me I could not make out why the horses were frightened.

Whilst we were talking, we heard a sort of sound between a yelp and a bark. It was far away; but the horses got very restless, and it took Johann all his time to quiet them. He was pale, and said, 'It sounds like a wolf—but yet there are no wolves here now.'

'No?' I said, questioning him; 'isn't it long since the wolves were so near the city?'

'Long, long,' he answered, 'in the spring and summer; but with the snow the wolves have been here not so long.'

Whilst he was petting the horses and trying to quiet them, dark clouds drifted rapidly across the sky. The sunshine passed away, and a breath of cold wind seemed to drift past us. It was only a breath, however, and more in the nature of a warning than a fact, for the sun came out brightly again. Johann looked under his lifted hand at the horizon and said:

'The storm of snow, he comes before long time.' Then he looked at his watch again, and, straightaway holding his reins firmly—for the horses were still pawing the ground restlessly and shaking their heads—he climbed to his box as though the time had come for proceeding on our journey.

I felt a little obstinate and did not at once get into the carriage.

'Tell me,' I said, 'about this place where the road leads,' and I pointed down.

Again he crossed himself and mumbled a prayer, before he answered, 'It is unholy.'

'What is unholy?' I enquired.

'The village.'

'Then there is a village?'

'No, no. No one lives there hundreds of years.' My curiosity was piqued, 'But you said there was a village.'

'There was.'

'Where is it now?'

Whereupon he burst out into a long story in German and English, so mixed up that I could not quite understand exactly what he said, but roughly I gathered that long ago, hundreds of years, men had died there and been buried in their graves; and sounds were heard under the clay, and when the graves were opened, men and women were found rosy with life, and their mouths red with blood. And so, in haste to save their lives (aye, and their souls!— and here he crossed himself) those who were left fled away to other places, where the living lived, and the dead were dead and not— not something. He was evidently afraid to speak the last words. As he proceeded with his narration, he grew more and more excited. It seemed as if his imagination had got hold of him, and he ended in a perfect paroxysm of fear—white-faced, perspiring, trembling and looking round him, as if expecting that some dreadful presence would manifest itself there in the bright sunshine on the open plain.

Finally, in an agony of desperation, he cried:

'Walpurgis Nacht!' and pointed to the carriage for me to get in. All my English blood rose at this, and, standing back, I said:

'You are afraid, Johann—you are afraid. Go home: I shall return alone; the walk will do me good.' The carriage door was open. I took from the seat my oak walking-stick—which I always carry on my holiday excursions—and closed the door, pointing back to Munich, and said, 'Go home, Johann—Walpurgis Nacht doesn't concern Englishmen.'

The horses were now more restive than ever, and Johann was trying to hold them in, while excitedly imploring me not to do anything so foolish. I pitied the poor fellow, he was deeply in earnest; but all the same I could not help laughing. His English was quite gone now. In his anxiety he had forgotten that his only means of making me understand was to talk my language, so he jabbered away in his native German. It began to be a little tedious. After giving the direction, 'Home!' I turned to go down the cross-road into the valley.

With a despairing gesture, Johann turned his horses towards Munich. I leaned on my stick and looked after him. He went slowly along the road for a while: then there came over the crest of the hill a man tall and thin. I could see so much in the distance. When he drew near the horses, they began to jump and kick about, then to scream with terror. Johann could not hold them in; they bolted down the road, running away madly. I watched them out of sight, then looked for the stranger, but I found that he, too, was gone.

With a light heart I turned down the side road through the deepening valley to which Johann had objected. There was not the slightest reason, that I could see, for his objection; and I daresay I tramped for a couple of hours without thinking of time or distance, and certainly without seeing a person or a house. So far as the place was concerned, it was desolation itself. But I did not notice this particularly till, on turning a bend in the road, I came upon a scattered fringe of wood; then I recognised that I had been impressed unconsciously by the desolation of the region through which I had passed.

I sat down to rest myself, and began to look around. It struck me that it was considerably colder than it had been at the commencement of my walk—a sort of sighing sound seemed to be around me, with, now and then, high overhead, a sort of muffled roar. Looking upwards I noticed that great thick clouds were drifting rapidly across the sky from north to south at a great height. There were signs of coming storm in some lofty stratum of the air. I was a little chilly, and, thinking that it was the sitting still after the exercise of walking, I resumed my journey.

The ground I passed over was now much more picturesque. There were no striking objects that the eye might single out; but in all there was a charm of beauty. I took little heed of time and it was only when the deepening twilight forced itself upon me that I began to think of how I should find my way home. The brightness of the day had gone. The air was cold, and the drifting of clouds high overhead was more marked. They were accompanied by a sort of far-away rushing sound, through which seemed to come at intervals that mysterious cry which the driver had said came from a wolf. For a while I hesitated. I had said I would see the deserted village, so on I went, and presently came on a wide stretch of open country, shut in by hills all around. Their sides were covered with trees which spread down to the plain, dotting, in clumps, the gentler slopes and hollows which showed here and there. I followed with my eye the winding of the road, and saw that it curved close to one of the densest of these clumps and was lost behind it.

As I looked there came a cold shiver in the air, and the snow began to fall. I thought of the miles and miles of bleak country I had passed, and then hurried on to seek the shelter of the wood in front. Darker and darker grew the sky, and faster and heavier fell the snow, till the earth before and around me was a glistening white carpet the further edge of which was lost in misty vagueness. The road was here but crude, and when on the level its boundaries were not so marked, as when it passed through the cuttings; and in a little while I found that I must have strayed from it, for I missed underfoot the hard surface, and my feet sank deeper in the grass and moss. Then the wind grew stronger and blew with ever increasing force, till I was fain to run before it. The air became icy-cold, and in spite of my exercise I began to suffer. The snow was now falling so thickly and whirling around me in such rapid eddies that I could hardly keep my eyes open. Every now and then the heavens were torn asunder by vivid lightning, and in the flashes I could see ahead of me a great mass of trees, chiefly yew and cypress all heavily coated with snow.

I was soon amongst the shelter of the trees, and there, in comparative silence, I could hear the rush of the wind high overhead. Presently the blackness of the storm had become merged in the darkness of the night. By-and-by the storm seemed to be passing away: it now only came in fierce puffs or blasts. At such moments the weird sound of the wolf appeared to be echoed by many similar sounds around me.

Now and again, through the black mass of drifting cloud, came a straggling ray of moonlight, which lit up the expanse, and showed me that I was at the edge of a dense mass of cypress and yew trees. As the snow had ceased to fall, I walked out from the shelter and began to investigate more closely. It appeared to me that, amongst so many old foundations as I had passed, there might be still standing a house in which, though in ruins, I could find some sort of shelter for a while. As I skirted the edge of the copse, I found that a low wall encircled it, and following this I presently found an opening. Here the cypresses formed an alley leading up to a square mass of some kind of building. Just as I caught sight of this, however, the drifting clouds obscured the moon, and I passed up the path in darkness. The wind must have grown colder, for I felt myself shiver as I walked; but there was hope of shelter, and I groped my way blindly on.

I stopped, for there was a sudden stillness. The storm had passed; and, perhaps in sympathy with nature's silence, my heart seemed to cease to beat. But this was only momentarily; for suddenly the moonlight broke through the clouds, showing me that I was in a graveyard, and that the square object before me was a great massive tomb of marble, as white as the snow that lay on and all around it. With the moonlight there came a fierce sigh of the storm, which appeared to resume its course with a long, low howl, as of many dogs or wolves. I was awed and shocked, and felt the cold perceptibly grow upon me till it seemed to grip me by the heart. Then while the flood of moonlight still fell on the marble tomb, the storm gave further evidence of renewing, as though it was returning on its track. Impelled by some sort of fascination, I approached the sepulchre to see what it was, and why such a thing stood alone in such a place. I walked around it, and read, over the Doric door, in German:

COUNTESS DOLINGEN OF GRATZ

IN STYRIA

SOUGHT AND FOUND DEATH

1801

On the top of the tomb, seemingly driven through the solid marble—for the structure was composed of a few vast blocks of stone—was a great iron spike or stake. On going to the back I saw, graven in great Russian letters:

'THE DEAD TRAVEL FAST.'

There was something so weird and uncanny about the whole thing that it gave me a turn and made me feel quite faint. I began to wish, for the first time, that I had taken Johann's advice. Here a thought struck me, which came under almost mysterious circumstances and with a terrible shock. This was Walpurgis Night!

Walpurgis Night, when, according to the belief of millions of people, the devil was abroad—when the graves were opened and the dead came forth and walked. When all evil things of earth and air and water held revel. This very place the driver had specially shunned. This was the depopulated village of centuries ago. This was where the suicide lay; and this was the place where I was alone—unmanned, shivering with cold in a shroud of snow with a wild storm gathering again upon me! It took all my philosophy, all the religion I had been taught, all my courage, not to collapse in a paroxysm of fright.

And now a perfect tornado burst upon me. The ground shook as though thousands of horses thundered across it; and this time the storm bore on its icy wings, not snow, but great hailstones which drove with such violence that they might have come from the thongs of Balearic slingers—hailstones that beat down leaf and branch and made the shelter of the cypresses of no more avail than though their stems were standing-corn. At the first I had rushed to the nearest tree; but I was soon fain to leave it and seek the only spot that seemed to afford refuge, the deep Doric doorway of the marble tomb. There, crouching against the massive bronze door, I gained a certain amount of protection from the beating of the hailstones, for now they only drove against me as they ricocheted from the ground and the side of the marble.

As I leaned against the door, it moved slightly and opened inwards. The shelter of even a tomb was welcome in that pitiless tempest, and I was about to enter it when there came a flash of forked-lightning that lit up the whole expanse of the heavens. In the instant, as I am a living man, I saw, as my eyes were turned into the darkness of the tomb, a beautiful woman, with rounded cheeks and red lips, seemingly sleeping on a bier. As the thunder broke overhead, I was grasped as by the hand of a giant and hurled out into the storm. The whole thing was so sudden that, before I could realise the shock, moral as well as physical, I found the hailstones beating me down. At the same time I had a strange, dominating feeling that I was not alone. I looked towards the tomb. Just then there came another blinding flash, which seemed to strike the iron stake that surmounted the tomb and to pour through to the earth, blasting and crumbling the marble, as in a burst of flame. The dead woman rose for a moment of agony, while she was lapped in the flame, and her bitter scream of pain was drowned in the thundercrash. The last thing I heard was this mingling of dreadful sound, as again I was seized in the giant-grasp and dragged away, while the hailstones beat on me, and the air around seemed reverberant with the howling of wolves. The last sight that I remembered was a vague, white, moving mass, as if all the graves around me had sent out the phantoms of their sheeted-dead, and that they were closing in on me through the white cloudiness of the driving hail.

*   *   *

Gradually there came a sort of vague beginning of consciousness; then a sense of weariness that was dreadful. For a time I remembered nothing; but slowly my senses returned. My feet seemed positively racked with pain, yet I could not move them. They seemed to be numbed. There was an icy feeling at the back of my neck and all down my spine, and my ears, like my feet, were dead, yet in torment; but there was in my breast a sense of warmth which was, by comparison, delicious. It was as a nightmare—a physical nightmare, if one may use such an expression; for some heavy weight on my chest made it difficult for me to breathe.

This period of semi-lethargy seemed to remain a long time, and as it faded away I must have slept or swooned. Then came a sort of loathing, like the first stage of sea-sickness, and a wild desire to be free from something—I knew not what. A vast stillness enveloped me, as though all the world were asleep or dead—only broken by the low panting as of some animal close to me. I felt a warm rasping at my throat, then came a consciousness of the awful truth, which chilled me to the heart and sent the blood surging up through my brain. Some great animal was lying on me and now licking my throat. I feared to stir, for some instinct of prudence bade me lie still; but the brute seemed to realise that there was now some change in me, for it raised its head. Through my eyelashes I saw above me the two great flaming eyes of a gigantic wolf. Its sharp white teeth gleamed in the gaping red mouth, and I could feel its hot breath fierce and acrid upon me.

For another spell of time I remembered no more. Then I became conscious of a low growl, followed by a yelp, renewed again and again. Then, seemingly very far away, I heard a 'Holloa! holloa!' as of many voices calling in unison. Cautiously I raised my head and looked in the direction whence the sound came; but the cemetery blocked my view. The wolf still continued to yelp in a strange way, and a red glare began to move around the grove of cypresses, as though following the sound. As the voices drew closer, the wolf yelped faster and louder. I feared to make either sound or motion. Nearer came the red glow, over the white pall which stretched into the darkness around me. Then all at once from beyond the trees there came at a trot a troop of horsemen bearing torches. The wolf rose from my breast and made for the cemetery. I saw one of the horsemen (soldiers by their caps and their long military cloaks) raise his carbine and take aim. A companion knocked up his arm, and I heard the ball whizz over my head. He had evidently taken my body for that of the wolf. Another sighted the animal as it slunk away, and a shot followed. Then, at a gallop, the troop rode forward—some towards me, others following the wolf as it disappeared amongst the snow-clad cypresses.

As they drew nearer I tried to move, but was powerless, although I could see and hear all that went on around me. Two or three of the soldiers jumped from their horses and knelt beside me. One of them raised my head, and placed his hand over my heart.

'Good news, comrades!' he cried. 'His heart still beats!'

Then some brandy was poured down my throat; it put vigour into me, and I was able to open my eyes fully and look around. Lights and shadows were moving among the trees, and I heard men call to one another. They drew together, uttering frightened exclamations; and the lights flashed as the others came pouring out of the cemetery pell-mell, like men possessed. When the further ones came close to us, those who were around me asked them eagerly:

'Well, have you found him?'

The reply rang out hurriedly:

'No! no! Come away quick—quick! This is no place to stay, and on this of all nights!'

'What was it?' was the question, asked in all manner of keys. The answer came variously and all indefinitely as though the men were moved by some common impulse to speak, yet were restrained by some common fear from giving their thoughts.

'It—it—indeed!' gibbered one, whose wits had plainly given out for the moment.

'A wolf—and yet not a wolf!' another put in shudderingly.

'No use trying for him without the sacred bullet,' a third remarked in a more ordinary manner.

'Serve us right for coming out on this night! Truly we have earned our thousand marks!' were the ejaculations of a fourth.

'There was blood on the broken marble,' another said after a pause—'the lightning never brought that there. And for him—is he safe? Look at his throat! See, comrades, the wolf has been lying on him and keeping his blood warm.'

The officer looked at my throat and replied:

'He is all right; the skin is not pierced. What does it all mean? We should never have found him but for the yelping of the wolf.'

'What became of it?' asked the man who was holding up my head, and who seemed the least panic-stricken of the party, for his hands were steady and without tremor. On his sleeve was the chevron of a petty officer.

'It went to its home,' answered the man, whose long face was pallid, and who actually shook with terror as he glanced around him fearfully. 'There are graves enough there in which it may lie. Come, comrades—come quickly! Let us leave this cursed spot.'

The officer raised me to a sitting posture, as he uttered a word of command; then several men placed me upon a horse. He sprang to the saddle behind me, took me in his arms, gave the word to advance; and, turning our faces away from the cypresses, we rode away in swift, military order.

As yet my tongue refused its office, and I was perforce silent. I must have fallen asleep; for the next thing I remembered was finding myself standing up, supported by a soldier on each side of me. It was almost broad daylight, and to the north a red streak of sunlight was reflected, like a path of blood, over the waste of snow. The officer was telling the men to say nothing of what they had seen, except that they found an English stranger, guarded by a large dog.

'Dog! that was no dog,' cut in the man who had exhibited such fear. 'I think I know a wolf when I see one.'

The young officer answered calmly: 'I said a dog.'

'Dog!' reiterated the other ironically. It was evident that his courage was rising with the sun; and, pointing to me, he said, 'Look at his throat. Is that the work of a dog, master?'

Instinctively I raised my hand to my throat, and as I touched it I cried out in pain. The men crowded round to look, some stooping down from their saddles; and again there came the calm voice of the young officer:

'A dog, as I said. If aught else were said we should only be laughed at.'

I was then mounted behind a trooper, and we rode on into the suburbs of Munich. Here we came across a stray carriage, into which I was lifted, and it was driven off to the Quatre Saisons—the young officer accompanying me, whilst a trooper followed with his horse, and the others rode off to their barracks.

When we arrived, Herr Delbrück rushed so quickly down the steps to meet me, that it was apparent he had been watching within. Taking me by both hands he solicitously led me in. The officer saluted me and was turning to withdraw, when I recognised his purpose, and insisted that he should come to my rooms. Over a glass of wine I warmly thanked him and his brave comrades for saving me. He replied simply that he was more than glad, and that Herr Delbrück had at the first taken steps to make all the searching party pleased; at which ambiguous utterance the maître d'hôtel smiled, while the officer pleaded duty and withdrew.

'But Herr Delbrück,' I enquired, 'how and why was it that the soldiers searched for me?'

He shrugged his shoulders, as if in depreciation of his own deed, as he replied:

'I was so fortunate as to obtain leave from the commander of the regiment in which I served, to ask for volunteers.'

'But how did you know I was lost?' I asked.

'The driver came hither with the remains of his carriage, which had been upset when the horses ran away.'

'But surely you would not send a search-party of soldiers merely on this account?'

'Oh, no!' he answered; 'but even before the coachman arrived, I had this telegram from the Boyar whose guest you are,' and he took from his pocket a telegram which he handed to me, and I read:

Bistritz.

Be careful of my guest—his safety is most precious to me. Should aught happen to him, or if he be missed, spare nothing to find him and ensure his safety. He is English and therefore adventurous. There are often dangers from snow and wolves and night. Lose not a moment if you suspect harm to him. I answer your zeal with my fortune.—*Dracula.*

As I held the telegram in my hand, the room seemed to whirl around me; and, if the attentive maître d'hôtel had not caught me, I think I should have fallen. There was something so strange in all this, something so weird and impossible to imagine, that there grew on me a sense of my being in some way the sport of opposite forces—the mere vague idea of which seemed in a way to paralyse me. I was certainly under some form of mysterious protection. From a distant country had come, in the very nick of time, a message that took me out of the danger of the snow-sleep and the jaws of the wolf.